HEALTH 2000

Purnell

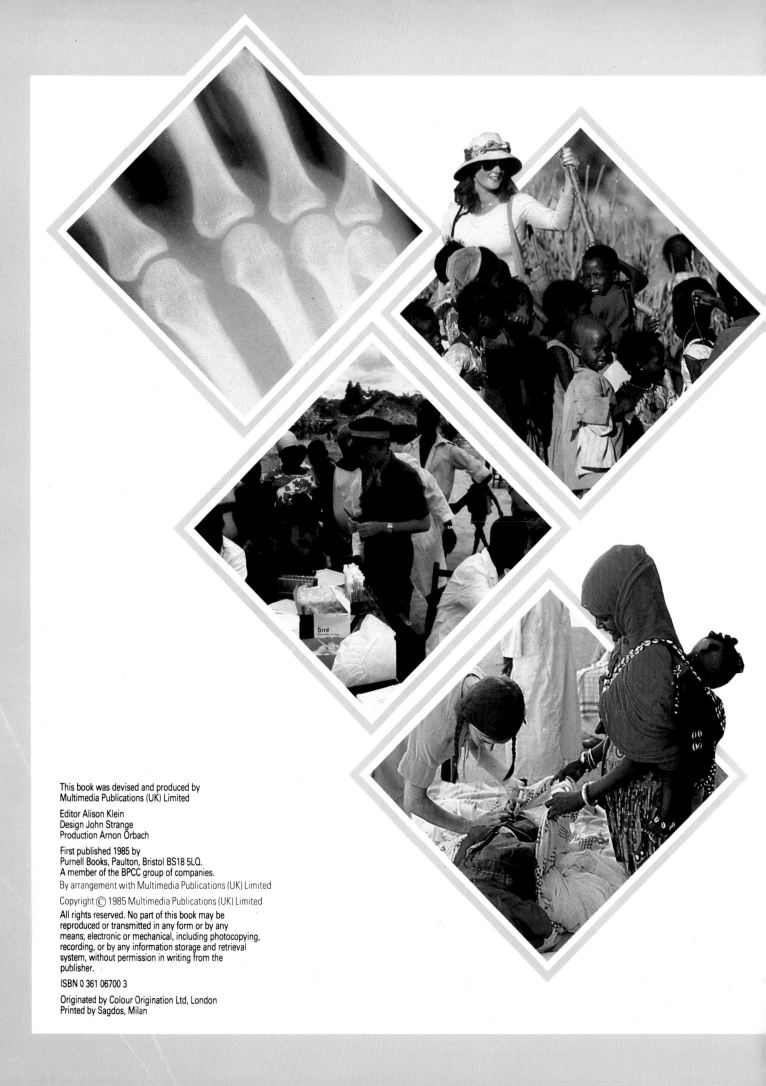

This book was devised and produced by
Multimedia Publications (UK) Limited

Editor Alison Klein
Design John Strange
Production Arnon Orbach

First published 1985 by
Purnell Books, Paulton, Bristol BS18 5LQ.
A member of the BPCC group of companies.

By arrangement with Multimedia Publications (UK) Limited

ISBN 0 361 06700 3

Originated by Colour Origination Ltd, London
Printed by Sagdos, Milan

CONTENTS

Foreword

Health is something we tend to ignore when we have it. When our body is working well, we're scarcely even aware of it. That's the way it should be.

But illness *can* come, even when we're young. In fact, through most of history, childhood has been a very dangerous time. Many diseases attacked children in particular and people knew very little about how to prevent such ailments or how to cure them once they struck. The result was that many children died.

About a century and a quarter ago, however, scientists found out about germs, and then everything changed. The cause of many diseases was discovered, and cures were developed. As this medical knowledge spread, the world became much safer for children.

Other discoveries were made about nutrition, about treatment in hospitals, about every aspect of health, as this book explains. The result is that whereas a hundred years ago the average person lived for 35 years, nowadays, in many parts of the world, people can expect to live for 75 years. That's 40 extra years.

And what do we expect by the year 2000? Undoubtedly, medical science will continue to advance. Some people will be able to avoid medical problems that are unavoidable today. But we can't expect everything to be perfect. New problems, new difficulties will arise. In fact, as this book makes clear, even when people are better off, *that* can give rise to illness, too. There is of course a lot that you can do to keep yourself healthy. What could be more important than your own body?

Isaac Asimov

Introduction

What is health?

Health is not a simple idea. For example, someone may be having medical treatment from a doctor or a hospital, yet still be healthier than a 'fit' person who is leading a very stressful, anxious life.

This book introduces you to the idea that a healthy life is a *good* life. Just what a good life actually is will become clear as you get to the end of the book. And you may find that some of the answers are not quite what you expected.

The book starts with a short description of how your body – the 'wonderful machine' – works. The working parts range in size from big muscles and bones to the tiny living cells that make up all parts of the body.

After this body survey, you will read how health and disease have affected peoples' minds and bodies throughout the age of modern medicine, which starts at the end of the 18th century and continues up to the present and beyond, to the year 2000.

Ron Taylor has written many articles and children's books on science and technology. For a number of years he was editor of two chemical technology journals and then of a twenty-volume science encyclopaedia. His particular interests are in the biosciences, including medicine. He has a degree in microbiology and has lectured in microecology. He has also published works of non-fiction and poetry.

Consultant editor Dr Robert Corringham

CHAPTER 1
The wonderful machine

Medical and health problems are the ones that affect peoples' bodies. So to understand these problems, you first have to know how your body works.

Your body is like a wonderful, complicated machine which you hope to keep in the very best working order. It has hundreds of times more different working parts than a complex machine such as a motor car. One of these parts, the brain, is itself far more complicated than even the biggest of today's computers. So how can you hope to understand the workings of the body at all?

Body systems
You can think of the human body machine as a number of different working systems, all of which are made up of several parts. Each system is then linked up with the others and together they make up the body's total operation.

The brain, together with all the nerves of the body that are connected to it, is one such system. This system is called the nervous system and it controls all the other systems of the body machine. Like all control systems, the nervous system works by messages. Electrical messages flow along your nerves to and from your brain and other organs, or working parts, of your body. For example, when you want to move your arm, electrical messages flow from your brain along nerves to the muscles in your arm. The muscles pull on your bones so that your arm moves in the way you want it to.

Many nerve messages are not as obvious as this. Once you have swallowed food, it is pushed down your digestive canal by muscles. But you do not have to think about this muscle action for it to happen. These automatic movements in your digestive system and other parts of the body are controlled by nerves that belong to a sub-system called the autonomic nervous system. This also controls such things as your blood pressure and body temperature, which are absolutely vital to life but which you hardly ever think about.

Muscles are the meat of the body. And bones make up the skeleton. These are both body systems, which together make up the body's framework.

Unconscious messages
The digestive system mentioned above can be thought of as the engine of the body. It uses food and drink as fuels — like the fuel of the motor car engine — to provide energy for the body.

◀ Robots are complicated man-made machines, but none, so far, has been made anything like as complicated as the human body machine. All robots are controlled from outside, but the body machine controls itself – and of course, can think about this control too.

Digestion really means breaking down or separating. To break down foods to simpler energy-providing substances, many special body chemicals are needed. These are made in the glands, the body's chemical factories. For the glands to work, they must first receive control messages. One message may tell a gland to start making a special chemical, while another message may tell it to stop.

As with body temperature and blood pressure, the messages that glands receive are unconscious ones, ones we do not have to think about. Many of these messages are of the kind we have already looked at: electrical messages flowing along nerves of the autonomic, or unconscious, nervous system. Many other messages, known as 'chemical messages', are chemicals made by glands themselves.

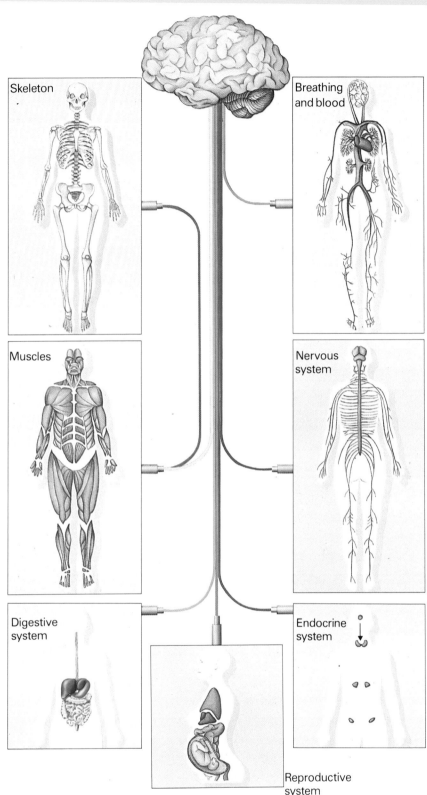

Skeleton

Breathing and blood

Muscles

Nervous system

Digestive system

Reproductive system

Endocrine system

▲
We eat to provide the body machine with fuel to make it work. Sugary food is easily burned or broken down in the body, to provide quick energy. Too much sugar, though, is converted into fat! Growing bodies also need protein food for building bone and muscle, plenty of vegetable fibre for good digestion, and fruit for its vitamins.

▲ The human body is entirely controlled by the brain. Through nerve messages, the brain tells the different parts of the body what is going on in them. The brain itself, together with all the nerves of the body, is a major body system. It controls all our activities, including the conscious ones such as thinking, speaking and walking, and also the unconscious or automatic ones, such as digesting and maintaining a normal balance and blood pressure. The brain also controls the endocrine-gland system which controls the production of hormones. These in turn control many body processes, including nervous ones. Together, nerves and hormones control other systems, such as sex and reproduction.

11

The wonderful machine

▲
'A beautifully controlled dive'. Such comments show that we often regard the body as a finely tuned machine.

These special control chemicals are called hormones and are carried about the body in the blood, to reach the organs they control. The sorts of glands that make hormones are known as endocrine glands, and taken all together they make up one more body system, called the endocrine system.

Dual control

So you can see that the body machine is really controlled in two ways: electrically and chemically. These two kinds of control work very closely together. For example, when you run a race, nerves carry messages to your muscles, telling them to work harder. But at the same time, a hormone called adrenaline flows in your blood to make your heart beat more strongly, to supply more energy-giving blood to your muscles.

Actually, the connection between the nervous system and the endocrine system is still closer. In this case, the adrenaline comes from glands which must first receive nerve messages in order to release their hormone into the blood.

Nerves and endocrine glands work closely together in the control of the body machine. But this is not the end of the complicated control story, because nerves themselves pass chemical messages as well as electrical ones. Chemicals made by nerves are called transmitters. They pass messages between one nerve and another that connects with it, and also between a nerve and the organ that it affects, such as a muscle.

In your brain, millions of these transmitter messages flow between nerve cells every second. Some of the latest medical drugs are chemicals that resemble or act upon these transmitters, so as to have a powerful action on the brain and also on the rest of the body. Such drugs can be very useful in treating illness. On the other hand, dangerous drugs such as heroin and morphine can also

▼ A lot is going on at the amusement park particularly in the minds and bodies of those enjoying themselves there. Even the first smell of hot dogs brings excitement and this is increased by the many thrills of the fairground machines. Dizziness at being whirled about, fear of leaving the safety of the solid ground, the excited shrieks of others, all add up to produce the expected fairground effect. In body-machine terms, the organs of balance deep in the ear are upset and make you dizzy and the hormone adrenaline flows faster in your blood making you feel excited.

affect transmitters, but in such a way as to cause the kind of illnesses we call addiction.

What's going on out there?
We have seen how chemical and electrical messages travel around in the body machine to control all its internal workings. All these instructions really come from the brain, because even the endocrine system which makes hormone messages is finally controlled by a part of the brain called the hypothalamus.

But of course, life does not carry on only inside your own body. What about messages from the outside world with which you are always in contact? You get these messages through your sense organs: eyes, ears, nose and mouth, and skin. They make it possible for you to see, hear, smell, taste and feel the world around you.

For example, if someone asks you a question, the sound message affects the nerves in your inner ear and they send electrical translations of the sound message to your brain. This then returns nerve messages and makes your muscles of speech work so that you can answer. The same sort of process goes on with other kinds of sense messages. Even while you are asleep, your body is still receiving these messages. Some people talk or even walk while they are asleep. So you can see that your body never 'shuts down' and 'switches off' completely.

Since your brain is always 'talking to your body', sense messages from the outside world to

The wonderful machine

your brain will often be passed on to your endocrine system and cause changes in its production of hormones. The runner we already mentioned is an example. He sees the runner in front of him, or the finishing line, and his increased flow of adrenaline gives him the thrust to try and win.

Other 'adrenaline emotions' are those of fear and anger, which can be aroused by something seen, heard or felt from outside. Sometimes they can occur just by thoughts happening in the mind. Other people often arouse strong feelings in us, and the more these people mean to us, the stronger our feelings are. One of the strongest personal bonds is between mother and baby. The picture shows how the messages that pass between these two include not only sense messages of sight, sound, smell and touch, but also several different hormone messages in the mother's body.

What your body is made of

So far we have looked at the body as a machine, seeing something of how it works. Just as an 'ordinary' machine has to be made from materials, such as metals and plastics, so the human body is made from materials, living tissues. One or another kind of living tissue makes up the main parts of the body.

Each different tissue is suited to its particular purposes in the body. Bone is a hard, strong tissue that can support the body's weight and stand up to quite strong stresses and knocks without damage. Muscles attached to bones also count as a tough, stress-resistant tissue, but they are springy so that body movements can be made.

Between the softer inner organs of the body, and protecting and supporting them, comes packing tissue. Some of this is fatty in texture — you will be able to find this sort easily enough, if you are overweight!

14   The organs themselves are

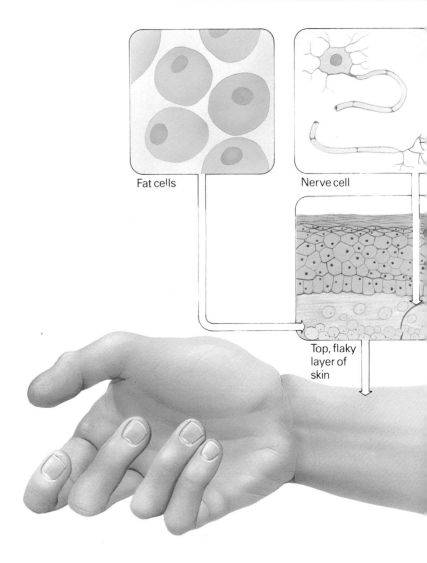

Fat cells

Nerve cell

Top, flaky layer of skin

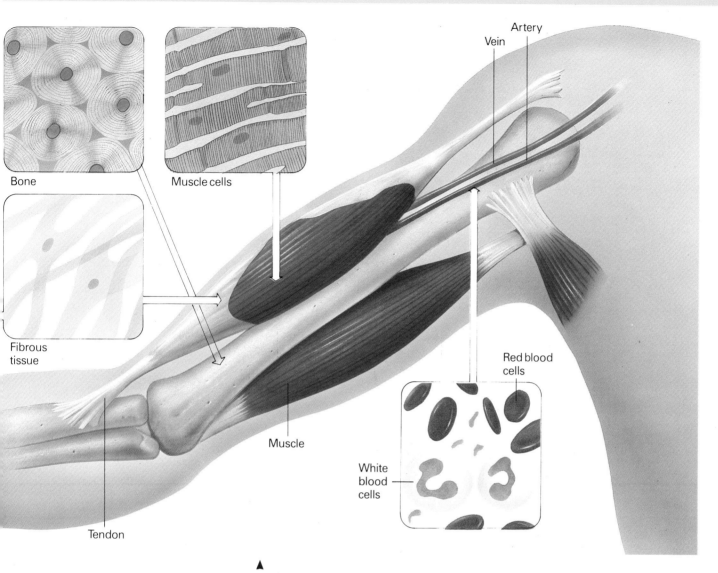

Bone

Muscle cells

Fibrous tissue

Vein

Artery

Red blood cells

Muscle

White blood cells

Tendon

◄ As the baby suckles it sends a message to its mother's brain. This tells her pituitary gland to release a hormone called prolactin which causes her breasts to make milk, and another hormone, oxytocin, which causes her breasts to release the milk.

▲
The brain controls this highly mobile part of the body through nerves leading to muscles, and also to some extent through hormones flowing in the blood. Tissues include the skin's several cell layers, ranging

from deeper, living cells to dead, flaky cells at the surface. Deeper still are fatty and fibrous layers, and below these, muscles. The picture on page 16 shows you more details of the structure of the skin.

made of several kinds of tissues, some of which we have met already, such as nervous tissue, which makes up brain and nerves, and glandular tissue. Lining tissues make up the surface layers of many organs, including glands. The skin, you may be surprised to know, counts as an organ of the body, and its outermost layer, the one you can see, is a living tissue.

All these living tissues are nourished by blood carried to them by blood vessels. A few tissues, such as hair and nails, get no blood supply and so are non-living tissues of the body.

Cells
Tissues make up the material or substance of the body — but what makes up tissues? The answer is cells, which are the units of living matter. Living cells are very small. To see them you will need the magnifying power of a microscope. This will show that human body cells have many different shapes.

Some, such as fat cells, are more or less round, while others such as muscle cells are longer and thinner. Nerve cells, or neurons, have very long, threadlike tails along which the nerves' electrical messages pass. Apart from having

different shapes, cells also have very different functions or duties. Gland cells are very 'busy' cells, making their special body chemicals like tiny factories.

So the body machine is really a supermachine because its smallest parts, living cells, are themselves complicated machines or factories. In the next section, we shall look at the body cells whose duties are defending your body against illness.

15

CHAPTER 2
Natural defences

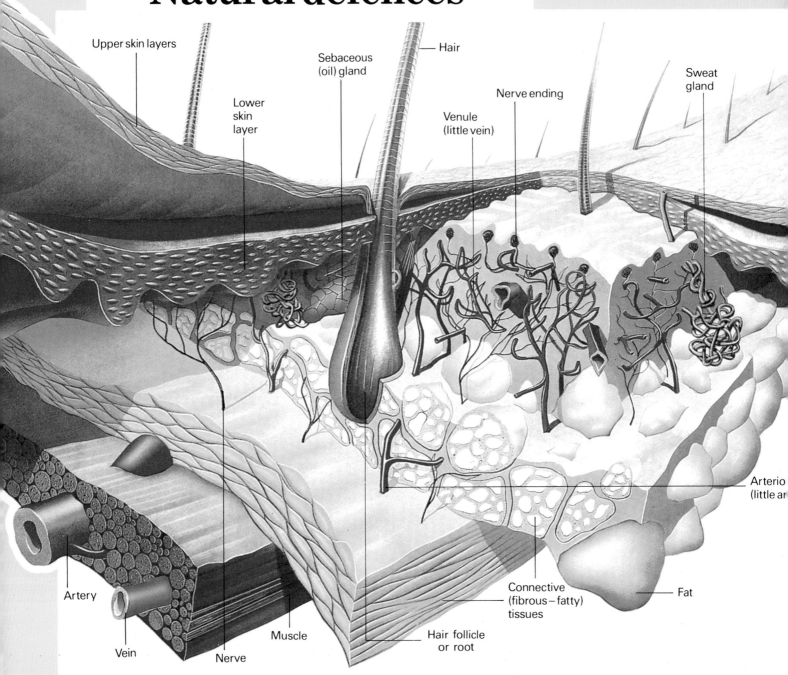

Upper skin layers

Lower skin layer

Sebaceous (oil) gland

Hair

Venule (little vein)

Nerve ending

Sweat gland

Artery

Vein

Nerve

Muscle

Hair follicle or root

Connective (fibrous–fatty) tissues

Fat

Arterio (little ar

To stay healthy you need to keep free from infection by harmful microbes. These microbes are tiny, living organisms and include disease-causing bacteria, viruses and other forms of microscopic life. They are far too small to be seen directly and can be carried into your body by the air you breathe, by food or drink, or perhaps through a cut or burn.

A very few microbes can get through unbroken skin. But this is an extremely rare way of catching an infection, for the very good reason that healthy skin is itself a protection or barrier against

disease. That is, your skin is one of your natural defences.

In the first place, skin is a complete covering which extends all over your body, even, though very thinly, over your eyes. Most microbes just cannot find a way through this barrier. Against those that keep trying, skin makes special bacteria-killing substances. Oily sebum made by the skin glands contains bacteria-killers and keeps skin naturally supple. Tears, made by eye glands, also contain bacteria-killers, helping further to protect these delicate organs. Ear wax helps guard

against bacteria, and urine too has an anti-bacterial action preventing infections of other very sensitive inner parts of the body.

Protective microbes
Now for a surprise. For all its defences, your skin actually swarms with bacteria!

These bacteria have learned to tolerate many of your skin's chemical weapons and they do not try particularly hard to get through into your blood. If they do get through, though, they can cause trouble.

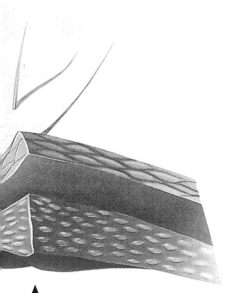

Skin is a complicated and versatile organ of the body, as its various layers and other parts show. It is a major defence barrier against infection. Very few microbes can get through skin to cause deeper harm, unless through a wound (see page 19). Many microbes do, however, live more or less harmlessly on its surface, including those in the hollows or follicles of hairs.

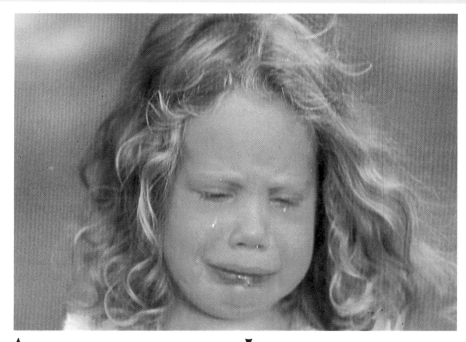

▲
Our skin defence barrier covers even our eyeballs, although here it is so thin as to be transparent. Tears not only wash the eye free of dust and grit, but also contain a chemical that kills any threatening microbes.

▼
The boxer's sweaty body shows another vital task of our skin covering. As the sweat evaporates from his skin, it takes away heat formed from his violent muscle action. Skin is our major organ of cooling.

Bacteria living on your skin are part of what is called your normal flora. (The word flora means flowers and biologists once considered the tiny bacteria to be distant relatives of plants such as flowers.) Your normal flora also includes many kinds of microbes living inside your nose and mouth and farther down in your intestines, in all of which places they are busy sharing your food.

But these normal-flora microbes are not simply idle lodgers. Some of them actually do useful work. For example, one common sort of bacterium helps make a vitamin that your body must have to stay healthy. Most of the huge number of normal-flora microbes, though, have one duty above all others — to keep rival microbes away.

These rivals are always about, waiting for a chance to settle and infect you with diseases because they are not adapted to your needs. They may multiply to cause dangerous infections. Very rarely this can happen because you are getting the latest in medical treatment. If you are

Natural defences

dosed too heavily with powerful antibiotic drugs, your normal flora may be killed off, allowing you to be colonized or settled by a yeast fungus, microscopic spores of which float about everywhere in the air. Dangerous fungal disease is just one result of harming the body's natural defences or immunity.

Defence in the blood

So what happens, exactly, if harmful microbes do manage to get through the body's outer defences and penetrate to where they can cause even more damage, in the blood and other inner tissues?

The answer is, of course, disease, if the invaders are not checked and are allowed to multiply freely. However, most invading microbes are checked, since we do not often develop an infectious disease. So if we are otherwise healthy, just how are the microbes checked?

The full answer to this question, a very complicated one indeed, is given by the science of immunology. One of the most valuable discoveries of immunology is vaccination against disease. This discovery was made two centuries ago and has since saved millions of lives (see page 20). But only in our own century has immunology become a true science and immunologists are still discovering new complications in the body's inner defences or immune system.

One thing can be said quite simply about this marvellous system of defence. It works mainly by the activities of white blood cells. These cells, which are less numerous than the red cells also contained in blood, are of several different kinds and have different defence duties. Among the best known are the phagocytes, white blood cells that wander about in the blood, gobbling up bacteria and other invaders that might cause harm.

But the phagocytes will only gobble up bacteria when helped to do so by further kinds of white blood cells, called lymphocytes, which are among the other main defence forces of the body. One type of lymphocyte, called the B lymphocyte, makes antibodies. Antibodies stick to the surface of any bacterium or other invader. Covered with antibodies, the invader can now be recognized by a phagocyte and gobbled up. Other kinds of antibodies act against the toxins or poisons made by bacteria, and so render them harmless.

This brief description of the immune system gives you some idea of the complex battle for health going on in the blood. The picture shows this battle in progress, with the addition of a few more units of the total defence forces, in a 'simple' case of infection, or inflammation, of the skin. It could in fact be called the Battle of the Boil!

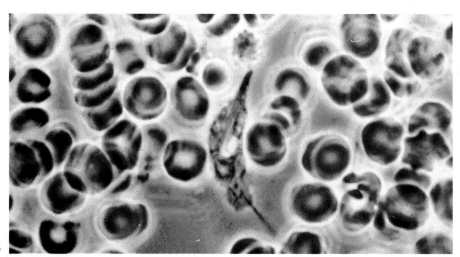

◀ Through the microscope, a real-life macrophage or active phagocyte (number 5 in the big picture above) can be seen in the middle of the picture, eating bacteria that have invaded the blood. The other cells are red blood cells.

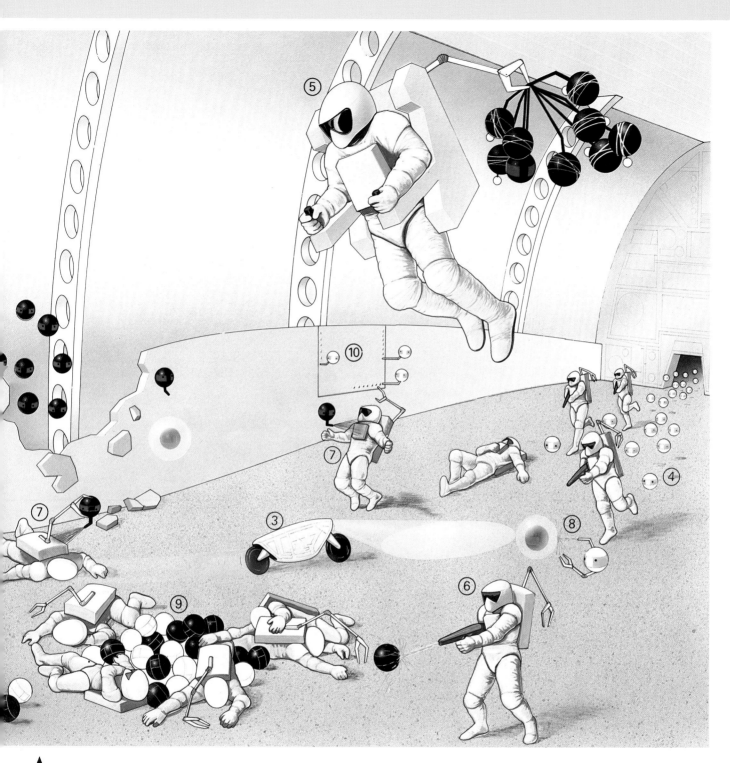

▲
The Battle of the Boil, or a simple case of skin inflammation, is shown here as a Space Invasion. First, invading bacteria get through a wound in the skin **1**. They produce substances that loosen or kill body cells, so allowing the infection to go deeper. **2**. But damaged cells release chemical messengers **3** which quickly summon aid. This comes mainly in the form of defensive white blood cells. Some of these are the white cells that produce antibodies which 'tie up' microbes so that they can do the body little more harm **4**. Other white cells are the phagocytes or microbe-eaters, which get rid of the invaders once they have been tied up with antibodies **5**, although some phagocytes can kill microbes directly with a substance called phagocytin **6**. The invading microbes, too, have their weapons, toxins or poisons that kill many body cells **7**. Some bacteria also resist phagocytes with defensive shields or capsules **8**. The debris created by the battle, dead white cells, bacteria and tissue cells, makes up the matter or pus that is typical of a 'ripe' boil or pimple **9**. Meanwhile, repair of damaged skin tissue is being carried out by further blood cells, including the tiny platelets **10** which help to produce the fibrous tissue or scab that plugs the wound and prevents further infection.

CHAPTER 3
A healthier world?

In the late 1700s, one in every five people living in London died from smallpox, a dreadful infectious disease. Even those that survived this terrible scourge were likely to be disfigured for life by the hundreds of deep pock-marks that pitted their faces.

After this time, smallpox became less and less of a killer in the cities, towns and villages of England. This relief was due to the pioneering work of one doctor, Edward Jenner. His great discovery can be said to have begun modern medicine. But what was this discovery?

Vaccination
Like many country people of his time, the young Jenner had noticed the clear complexion of milkmaids working on local farms. This meant, of course, that the milkmaids did not often suffer from smallpox. But they often caught a mild disease, called cowpox, from the cows they tended. This disease produced watery blisters or vesicles on the skin, which soon disappeared without further trouble.

Jenner the doctor saw what other people had failed to see — that the mild disease cowpox somehow protected the milkmaids against the severe disease smallpox. In 1796 he scratched liquid from a cowpox vesicle into the arm of a boy, then a few months later injected into the same boy the deadly substance that had filled a smallpox vesicle. The boy did not develop smallpox and stayed perfectly healthy.

Jenner's discovery of vaccination, as the scratching treatment was called (after the Latin word *vacca* meaning cow) turned out a boon to the whole of humanity, because smallpox is now a very rare disease in all parts of the world. Even so, it has taken nearly two centuries for Jenner's gift to reach the peoples of many poor tropical countries, who only recently have been freed from the threat of death or disfigurement from smallpox.

Modern immunization
Vaccination is just one kind of immunization. Today, doctors immunize us against many other infectious diseases besides smallpox. In fact, because smallpox is so very rare, we don't often need to be immunized against it, although many of the inoculations we receive as babies, or when travelling abroad, are still called vaccines.

▶ People were first protected against smallpox with inoculation of a liquid from the watery blisters of a mild disease caught from cows. This is how we get the word vaccination, from the Latin word *vacca* meaning cow. The cartoonist Gillray made gruesome fun of these early vaccinations by showing cows breaking out from various places on people's bodies.

▼
A tourist enjoys a meeting with African villagers. Infectious diseases in Africa are still so common that tourists need the protection of several inoculations before they set out on their tour. What is not realized quite so readily, is that Africans also need these protective inoculations, but all too often do not get them.

The Diseases and Casualties this Week.

Disease	Count	Disease	Count
		Imposthume	11
		Infants	16
		Killed by a fall from the Belfrey at Alhallows the Great	1
		Kingsevil	2
		Lethargy	1
		Palsie	1
		Plague	7165
Abortive	5	Rickets	17
Aged	43	Rising of the Lights	11
Ague	2	Scowring	5
Apoplexie	1	Scurvy	2
Bleeding	1	Spleen	1
Burnt in his Bed by a Candle at St. Giles Cripplegate	1	Spotted Feaver	101
		Stilborn	17
Canker	1	Stone	2
Childbed	42	Stopping of the stomach	9
Chrisomes	18	Strangury	1
Consumption	134	Suddenly	1
Convulsion	64	Surfeit	49
Cough	2	Teeth	121
Dropsie	33	Thrush	5
Feaver	309	Timpany	1
Flox and Small-pox	5	Tissick	11
Frighted	3	Vomiting	3
Gowt	1	Winde	3
Grief	3	Wormes	15
Griping in the Guts	51		
Jaundies	5		

Christned { Males	95	Buried { Males	4095	Plague — 7165
Females	81	Females	4202	
In all	176	In all	8297	

Increased in the Burials this Week ———— 607
Parishes clear of the Plague ——— 4 Parishes Infected ——— 126

The Assize of Bread set forth by Order of the Lord Mayor and Court of Aldermen, A penny Wheaten Loaf to contain Nine Ounces and a half, and three half-penny White Loaves the like weight.

▲
This 'Bill of Mortality' of 1665, the year of the Great Plague, shows how many people died and of what, in London, in the week ending September 26.

Doctor Jenner's discovery was in some ways a hundred years before its time. His vaccine, like all more recent vaccines, worked because it increased greatly the number of protective antibodies in the patient's blood. Antibodies, as we have seen already (pages 18–19), attack and help destroy disease microbes in the blood. But Jenner knew little of disease microbes, which were only recognized by doctors almost a century later. He also knew nothing at all of antibodies, which are a 20th-century discovery. But he did know that his vaccine worked! This delay in discovery explains why immunology is a 20th-century medical science, and not a 19th-century one.

19th-century plagues

In Western countries, the 19th century was not particularly unhealthy, when compared with the centuries that came before it. This is certainly no recommendation for that century, because if a family of today could be transported back to it, mother, father and children would all be terrified by the threat of infectious disease.

Thanks to Jenner's discovery, smallpox was a dwindling plague by the late 19th century. Other infectious diseases, equally deadly, were still raging. Children no longer died of starvation, as so many had in Europe up to the end of the 18th century, but they were all too likely to die from the attacks of typhoid, typhus, scarlet fever, diphtheria or even measles. If they did survive these diseases to grow up, their adult lives were often cut short by tuberculosis, the biggest killer of all at the end of the 19th century.

Compare the health situation today. Living in one of the better-off countries, you probably will not know of a single person suffering from any of these diseases (except possibly measles), much less dying from one. So what has conquered these killers of yesterday?

A healthier world?

The great doctors

The 19th-century doctors certainly had a great deal to do with it. Greatest of these was the Frenchman Louis Pasteur. To know what Pasteur achieved, we must first understand what exactly science knew about microbes by the mid-19th century.

Bacteria, small enough to be heaped in thousands on the point of a pin, had been known for three centuries but were still largely a mystery. Many scientists believed that these tiniest and simplest forms of life just came about from non-living matter. Pasteur showed that they did not do so, but were creatures that lived, reproduced and died like other, far larger creatures. He thus removed much superstition from thoughts about microbial life.

Neither did scientists know what part, if any, bacteria played in disease. Pasteur showed that they could infect and spoil food and drink, so almost certainly could also infect and cause disease in animals and humans. The 'certainly' was provided by the slightly later work of a German country doctor, Robert Koch. He proved that particular bacteria cause particular diseases. Koch and Pasteur went on to identify several disease bacteria and to grow these in their laboratories. These were the first vital steps to finding cures for bacterial disease, one of the world's greatest scourges before our own century.

Louis Pasteur is also immortal in medical history for his vaccine against rabies, a disease from which nearly all previous human sufferers had died horribly. This and Pasteur's other vaccines were the first since Jenner's smallpox vaccine 90 years previously.

Pasteur's new discovery was even greater than you might think. Rabies, like smallpox, is caused by a virus, a type of microbe smaller even than the smallest bacterium. Like Jenner before him, Pasteur could not see the cause of the disease he was

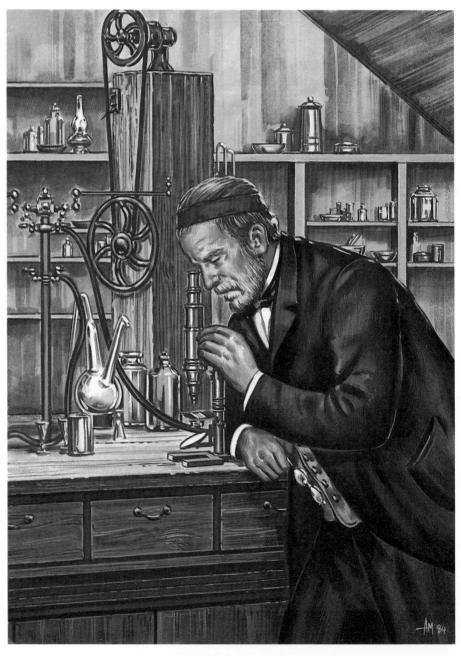

◄ A mad dog is a terrifying sight. Before Louis Pasteur's time it was doubly terrifying, because there was then no protection against rabies, a fatal virus disease caught from the bites of infected dogs and other animals. Pasteur developed a vaccine that successfully prevented the disease developing, if given before or soon after the bite.

► Measles is another viral disease against which we can be protected by a vaccine. For this reason, few children in richer countries now suffer badly from measles. But many unprotected children in poorer countries still suffer or even die.

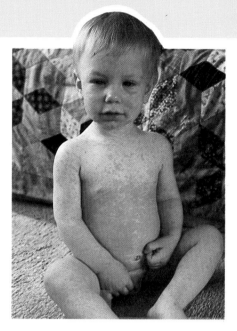

▼ Robert Koch (*left*) and Louis Pasteur showed for certain that microbes can cause disease. Koch, who discovered the germs of several major diseases, carried out the important experiment shown. He took blood from diseased cattle, injected this into mice, which also developed the disease, then grew or cultured the bacteria responsible in laboratory test tubes. From these he infected healthy cattle, which developed the same disease. He had shown that a particular kind of bacterium causes a particular disease.

◄ Louis Pasteur, famous chemist and bacteriologist, in his laboratory.

treating, because viruses are much too small for the microscopes of his day. But unlike Jenner, he knew they were there, and his vaccine, prepared from a specially weakened form of the virus, was the first of the wide range of powerful anti-virus vaccines we have today.

Safer, cleaner operations

Just after Pasteur made his discoveries about the cause of infectious disease, hospitals in his and other Western countries became safer places. These two great leaps forward in medical science are linked together, but to see just how and why we shall have to go back to the earlier 19th century.

Hospitals of the time were dirty, unhygienic places and patients were often lucky to get out alive. Ignorant of the fact that dirt and its microbes carried disease, doctors and nurses as often as not caused outbreaks of infections rather than cured them. One in ten pregnant women unfortunate enough to have her baby in such a hospital could expect to die after giving birth, from the violently painful infection known as child-bed fever. This, most likely, had been carried to her body by a surgeon who had come straight from the hospital dissecting rooms without washing his hands, or by a midwife who in any case rarely washed hers.

One surgeon at such a 'lying-in' hospital had become convinced that the fatal child-bed fever was carried in this way. Ignaz Semmelweiss, a Hungarian working in Vienna, tried to persuade his medical colleagues to wash their hands thoroughly before touching a surgical patient or a woman giving birth. His good advice not only went unrewarded but he was driven out of hospital, job and country by fellow doctors enraged at what they saw as a wicked slur on their profession.

Only a few years later, Louis Pasteur showed just how and why 23

A healthier world?

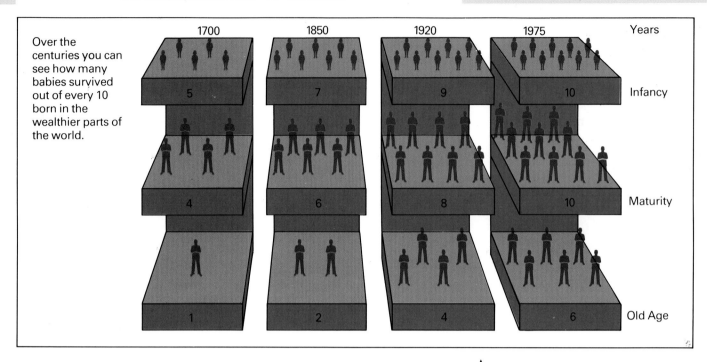

Over the centuries you can see how many babies survived out of every 10 born in the wealthier parts of the world.

	1700	1850	1920	1975	Years
Infancy	5	7	9	10	
Maturity	4	6	8	10	
Old Age	1	2	4	6	

dirty hands could carry child-bed fever and other infections. At this time, another important doctor came on the scene, the Scottish surgeon Joseph Lister.

Semmelweiss had not known that bacteria cause infectious disease, yet had some notion of antiseptics, liquids that prevent poisonous or septic infections. He had asked his irate fellow surgeons to cleanse their hands in chlorine water, which is a fairly effective germ-destroyer. Joseph Lister, quick off the mark to put Pasteur's discovery to hospital use, invented a device which sprayed a stronger antiseptic, carbolic acid, so killing any disease germs in the surrounding air.

Together with more scrupulous cleanliness of surgeons and nurses, this changed surgical operations completely for the better. Instead of the likelihood of painful infection often followed by death, a surgical patient could now look forward to speedy recovery as his infection-free wound healed itself.

Lister's antiseptic operating room killed off bacteria in or around the wound. From there it was just one step, though a large and important one, to the aseptic operating conditions of today's

hospitals. These environments are completely safe and kept free from bacteria and dirt at all times.

Surgery without pain

Another feature of today's surgical operations is that they are painless. The operations carried out in earlier centuries look more like mutilating forms of torture. A surgeon of those days was likely to be most famous for the speed at which he could cut off an arm or leg or extract a diseased organ. This was for the very good reason that there were no anaesthetics or other pain killers to be had beyond a strong dose of rum or other stupefying potion that could be forced on the patient.

Under such a surgical ordeal, a luckless patient might well die of shock even before he had time to develop the infection that would

▲
In our century, more people reach old age, as the picture shows. The reason is partly modern medicine, but mostly better food and cleaner living conditions.

otherwise have carried him off.

Even minor operations, such as the removal of a tooth, could cause prolonged agony without anaesthetics. It was the avoidance of such agony that led an American dentist, Horace Wells, to experiment with laughing gas in 1844, using himself as a guinea

► Joseph Lister operates with the aid of his carbolic acid spray. This made surgical operations safer, because the spray killed any disease microbes near the surgical wound.

▼
Anaesthetics are a great boon to modern life because they relieve pain. They were first used by a dentist of the early 19th century to put patients to sleep, to relieve the pain of surgical operations.

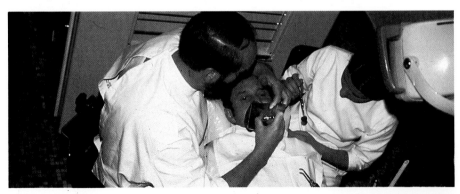

24

pig. This gas, called more scientifically nitrous oxide, causes a light sleep or anaesthesia when breathed in, yet one deep enough for painless tooth extractions.

Wells' bold experiment was soon followed by many others and performed by surgeons of various countries, during which stronger anaesthetics were discovered and tested. These included the gas ether and the liquid chloroform. Using them, surgeons could keep their patients unconscious and free from pain through operations that might last up to many hours.

Such operating times were almost unthinkable before the use of the anaesthetics. Because patients no longer struggled constantly against pain, the surgeons had the time and opportunity to improve their techniques and to carry out ever more complicated surgery with an ever greater record of success. Which is, of course, just what we expect of surgeons and surgery today.

A healthier world?

The long road to health

So far, the story of modern health and medicine has been one of famous doctors and their discoveries. Of course, these will always be important to medicine, simply because doctors are the people most committed to spend their time and talents trying to solve particular medical problems. But as you will see elsewhere in this book, most of the really big health problems are beyond the power of any one doctor to solve. They are problems that can only be tackled by whole communities of people, working together under enlightened governments, in countries that have wealth and resources enough to provide good health care for everyone.

Many industrial cities in the early 19th century were almost the exact opposite of this. Factories were springing up everywhere to fill the air with harmful fumes. Poverty-stricken people from the surrounding countryside were flocking into the cities to work long, exhausting and underpaid hours in the factories. As the city populations boomed, their places of living became more and more overcrowded and unhealthy. Whole families of workpeople crammed into each room of houses that had been bad to start with. Without toilets, proper drains or any form of garbage collection, these soon became filthy and evil-smelling slums. Their wretched inhabitants ate bad food, drank dirty water and breathed in air loaded with soot and germs.

Such terrible conditions of life greatly increased the chance of epidemic infections. For a century or more, the 'Asiatic cholera' had been reaching into Europe from countries farther east. This fatal bowel infection caused its sufferers to lose so much body fluid that they were reduced to living skeletons in a matter of hours. In 1848, more than 70,000 English and Welsh people died of cholera and other bowel infections, mainly in the towns and cities.

26

◀◀ The picture of downtown Hong Kong shows how many people still have to live in this rich but crowded city. Life on a floating sampan or junk may be very picturesque to the eyes of tourists, but in such crowded conditions, with everyone's garbage also floating around, it can be very unhealthy too.

◀ Tenements in Glasgow, Scotland, photographed in about 1868, show a scene which was just as crowded and unhealthy. Tenements such as these were often left unimproved until quite recently.

This frightful toll led one English doctor, John Snow, to take the unusual action of removing the handle of the pump in one central London district, so cutting off the main drinking water supply to that crowded and dirty city area. Its citizens had to go elsewhere for their water — but deaths from cholera began to fall off almost immediately. John Snow had confirmed what many less bold doctors had long suspected — that cholera epidemics were caused by infectious material from open sewers leaking into the water supply and being carried by it from place to place and person to person.

Obviously, if clean water could be provided, then cholera epidemics could not happen. Within a few years, the governments of several civilized countries had woken up to this fact, but it was not until the end of the 19th century that most European cities could boast a clean water supply. The task of supplying safe water to a large city was by no means an easy or simple one.

Sewage and sanitation

First, drains and sewers had to be built underground to carry away the human wastes that could harbour infections. In the larger cities this took many years of engineering work, after which, as often as not, wastes from sewers were allowed to flow into local rivers, so continuing to be a menace to health! Only in the 20th

27

A healthier world?

century was sewage made completely harmless in large sewage treatment plants. Indoor toilets with an efficient flush were also largely a development of the early 20th century.

After sewers, the next greatest need was a method for checking that water supplies were free from infection. This could only be done when the real causes of water-borne diseases were discovered. One step forward occurred in 1883, when Robert Koch identified the bacterium that causes cholera. At about the same time, another

► Clean water is a must for health. The far picture shows a rusty drum which contains the only water supply for a Sudanese village. Compare this with the clean, hot water used in a modern kitchen.

▼ Water from lakes, rivers or wells needs to be purified before it can be supplied to homes, factories or offices for drinking purposes. The picture shows how this is done. Town and factory get their drinking water from an underground reservoir. This water has been purified and freed from all bacteria in a large water-treatment plant, where most bacteria are filtered out and the remaining few killed by chlorine or ozone gas. Village water from a well, which contains fewer bacteria, is usually chlorinated or ozonated before it is supplied to taps.

Ⓟ Pumping stations

Ⓦ Artesian well

Ⓕ Filters

Ⓒ Chlorine treatment

Ⓞ Ozone treatment

Ⓤ Underground reservoir

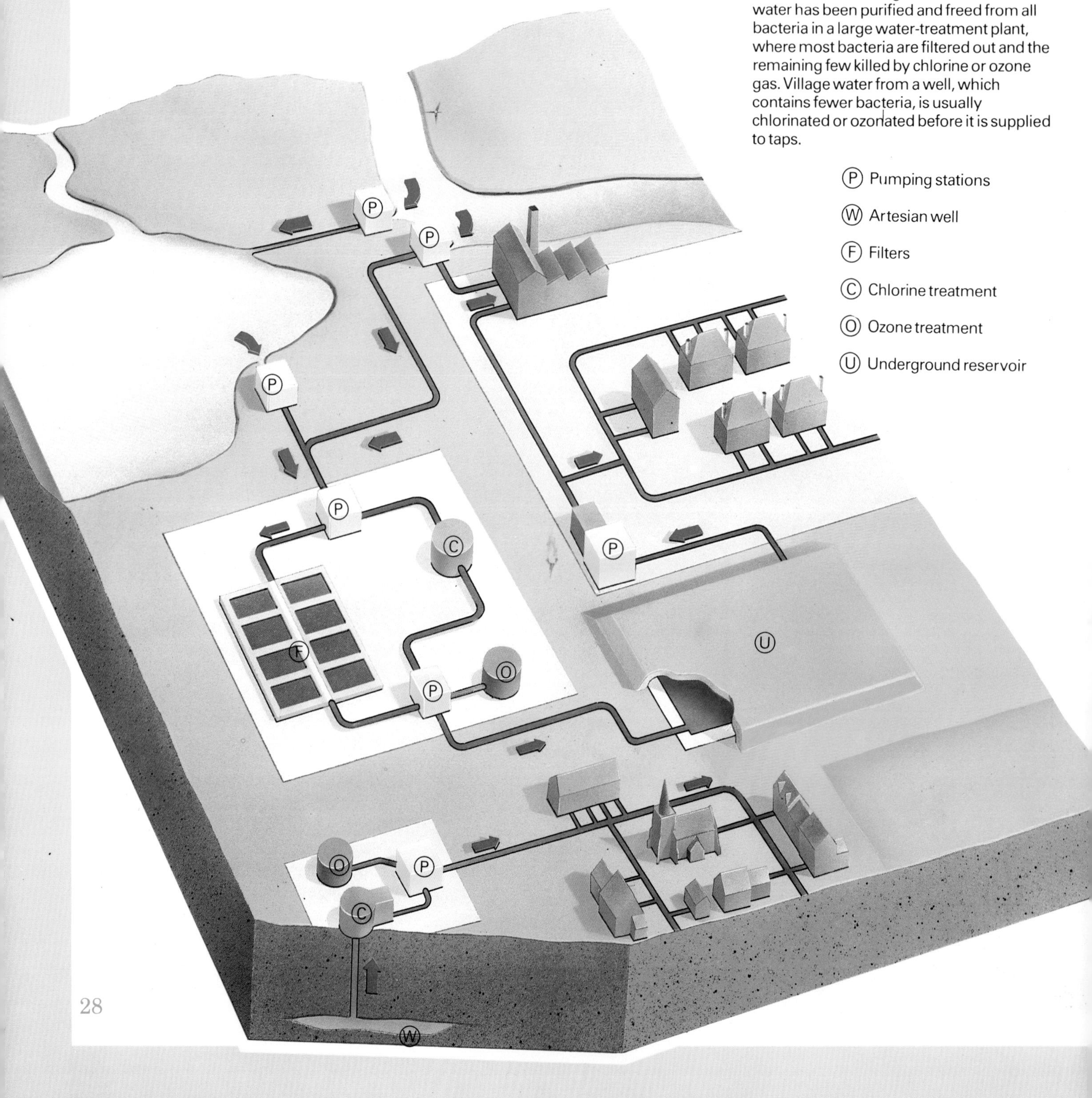

scientist discovered the bacterium that causes typhoid fever, the next greatest killer among water-borne diseases of the cities. Now that the culprits were known, they could be attacked. In our own century, our drinking water is made absolutely safe in water treatment plants which kill off all bacteria before the water is supplied to our household taps.

Where it hasn't happened
Safe water, better food and housing, and efficient medical attention when needed has proved to be the formula for a longer and healthier life in many countries.

But in many others, including those countries with the most people, these improvements have not yet happened. Despite the great advances of modern science and technology, more of which you can read about in the next section, tens of millions of poorer people in many of the great cities of the world still suffer living conditions as bad in most ways as those of the poor of the 19th century.

Tuberculosis or TB, once the greatest killer of all in Western countries but now a rare disease, is still a very frequent cause of death in the poorer countries of Africa, South America and Asia. Better food and less crowded housing played the biggest part in ridding the West of this infectious plague, but these benefits have yet to reach sufferers in the hot, poorer countries. TB has become just another 'tropical disease'.

We in the richer countries now feel secure from those old enemies of mankind, the epidemic disease bacteria, but most of mankind can feel no such comfort. Until it does, we cannot really give a positive answer to the question 'Do we live in a healthier world?'

◀ In the African countryside, clean water is often a luxury. People have to get their washing and drinking water from lakes and rivers. Sometimes this leads to the spread of disease.

CHAPTER 4
Medical miracles

In the 1880s, a young chemist began work at Robert Koch's medical research institute in Germany. Already he had invented a staining method that had helped Koch to identify the bacterium causing tuberculosis, one of the greatest enemies of mankind.

The young chemist's name was Paul Ehrlich, and he went on to make many other discoveries, chief of which was chemotherapy. This is the use of special chemicals, made mostly in the laboratory, for the treatment of disease. A few man-made drugs, such as aspirin, were already known at this time, but most medical drugs were extracted from plants, as they still are in traditional Chinese medicine.

Ehrlich's drugs had a much more direct and understandable effect than most of these natural extracts. This led to the most famous one, salvarsan, being known as the 'magic bullet' because it went straight to its target. Salvarsan was the first really effective drug cure for the venereal disease syphilis, and also for yaws, a widespread tropical ulcerating disease. Ehrlich also developed some of the first antiserums, drugs made from antibodies that attack bacteria or neutralize their poisons. His antiserum against diphtheria led, eventually, to the end of this disease, one of the most feared child killers.

The drug industry
Ehrlich's chemotherapy, with its strictly scientific and exact drug preparations, paved the way for the growth of the world's largest medical industry - all those factories and research laboratories that make the thousands of different drugs we so rely upon today. There can be no doubt that these drugs have changed our lives for the better. Not only are syphilis and yaws no longer the killers that they were, but most other diseases caused by microbes such as

bacteria and fungi are now quickly treatable, usually with complete cure. The once-fatal diphtheria, epidemic meningitis and lobar pneumonia are among bacterial diseases that have almost disappeared in developed countries, mainly because of chemotherapy.

Meningitis and pneumonia were overcome with the aid of sulpha drugs, first made in laboratories around 1930. These were the most powerful and widely acting man-made drugs before penicillin. Because they are so effective against bacteria, they helped put an end to many epidemics. There were no longer so many disease microbes about to cause these epidemics and so the pattern of infectious disease in many countries began to improve rapidly.

Sulpha drugs are still counted as useful chemical weapons today, but they do have a major drawback — one which they share with many other modern drugs. Besides being such powerful cures, at the same time they are fairly

drastic poisons! Bacteria and fungi are, after all, living cells, so that any substance which poisons them so effectively is bound to do some harm to other kinds of living cells, including our own.

Antibiotics
The search for less poisonous drugs than salvarsan and the sulpha drugs led to the discovery of the antibiotics. These are the most widely used of anti-microbial drugs of today and in a way, are just as much natural products as the old plant extracts had been. They, too, are produced by living creatures as part of their natural ways of life. But the anti-bacterial and anti-fungal substances known as antibiotics are made by the living bacteria and fungi themselves, for the purpose of discouraging the growth of other, rival microbes. And because they are made in and by living cells, and not by non-living chemical processes, antibiotics are in general less poisonous than sulpha drugs or salvarsan.

◄ A sore throat is soon cured with an antibiotic. Earlier in the 20th century, before the discovery of these powerful drugs, a sore throat could be much more sinister. It could mean the start of a severe infection such as diphtheria. These killers are now rare in countries where penicillin and other antibiotics are prescribed by doctors to most people. Unfortunately this is still not true of those poor countries, where only rich people can afford proper antibiotic treatment.

► Antibiotic drugs are big business in affluent countries. Every day, many thousands of bottles and packets are filled with these drugs in pharmaceutical factories.

▼ This medicine shop, in the Loang People's Commune of China, contains no antibiotic drugs. But China holds the world's longest record for drug treatment of illnesses. Each one of the many bottles holds some special preparation from plant, insect or animal. Chinese drug books contain tens of thousands of recipes for such drugs.

Medical miracles

The discovery of penicillin is one of the most famous of modern scientific detective stories. In 1928, Alexander Fleming noticed that many of the disease bacteria growing on one of his laboratory 'culture plates' had been killed off. He traced their killers to one or more equally tiny spores of the common blue or green fungus mould named *Penicillium*. These had floated through the air to land on his culture plate and grown there. In the early 1940s, Howard Florey and Ernst Chain succeeded in growing this mould in large quantities and in extracting from it the antibiotic called penicillin, which has since saved many millions of lives.

Penicillin is such an effective drug because it prevents the growth of many disease bacteria, while doing little harm to human or animal cells. A few people, though, cannot be given penicillin, because their immune system (see page 18) makes them extremely sensitive to, or easily damaged by, the drug. What is true for penicillin goes also for other antibiotics. Some of these, including the almost equally famous streptomycin, are rather more poisonous and so cannot be given quite so freely or in such large doses.

In general, where one antibiotic will not get rid of a 'bug' then another one will. So for many infections nowadays, we are given either this antibiotic or that one, or perhaps a 'cocktail' of several different antibiotics which see off several kinds of bug all at once. This cocktail may also be necessary because a particular troublesome bug has learned to fight back! If some bacteria and fungi make antibiotics to stop others growing, then the victim microbes may be expected, given time, to make natural antidotes or defence weapons against the antibiotics. This is, indeed, just what is happening on an ever-growing scale, as more and more antibiotics tablets are given out by doctors or bought from the chemists' shelves.

▼
This baby is in intensive care, in which all aspects of its health are recorded or monitored. Also, the baby may be dosed regularly with exact amounts of antibiotics or other drugs.

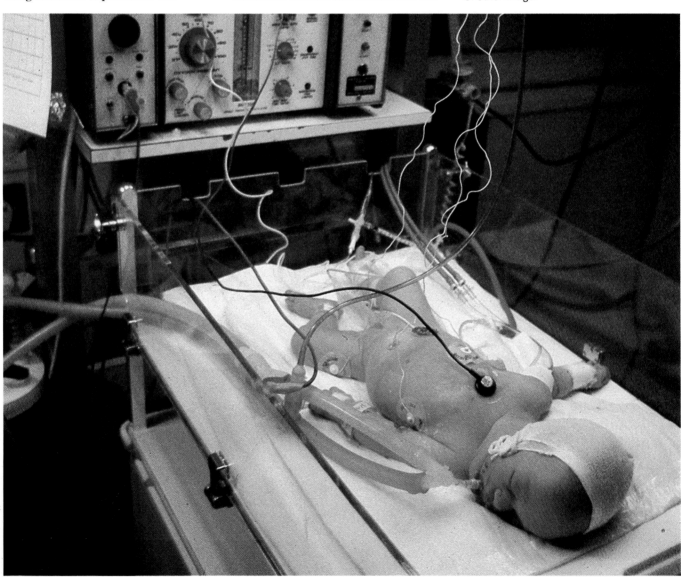

Just how have the microbes learned to fight back? To answer this question, we must see what happens as microbes grow in our bodies to cause disease.

Microbes and genes

Quite probably you have heard someone refer to the genes they inherited from their father or mother: the genes for their eye colour or for tallness or shortness. You may also know already that the genes are contained on chromosomes. Chromosomes are small parts of the cells of our bodies, including those special cells concerned with reproduction, the man's sperm and the woman's eggs or ova.

Microbes, too, have genes that they pass on to their offspring, and as with ourselves, the microbe's genes are what decide all its different properties and characteristics. Being much simpler organisms than ourselves, microbes have many fewer genes. But even a simple organism such as a bacterium will still have a good many genes. These are usually contained on a single chromosome. The chromosome is shaped like a tangled loop or necklace, along which the genes are strung like beads.

▼
Penicillin, most powerful of all antibiotic drugs, is obtained from a blue or green mould similar to the one often found growing on stale bread.

▲
Genes are the parts of each of the cells of our bodies, that make us what we are. This girl, for example, gets her green eyes and freckles from genes handed down, like all her other genes, from her parents.

▼
Cells of bacteria that live harmlessly in our intestines, magnified about 10,000 times. Each bacterial cell contains a single chromosome, a tangled loop that contains all the bacterium's genes.

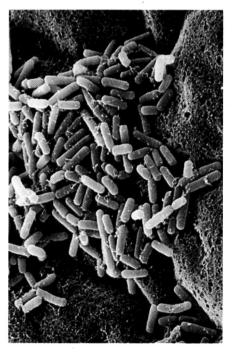

Medical miracles

Now, when disease bacteria in the body are exposed to an antibiotic, most of them will be killed off or stopped from reproducing. Just a few, however, may survive. These are the ones with genes for resistance to the antibiotic. They may soon re-multiply, until they reach such numbers that they can again cause disease. And because they are now all resistant, the antibiotic will have no further effect on them.

In such a bad case, the doctor will have to try another antibiotic, but this also may not work because the bacteria may have genes to resist this one too. Some bacteria, including some descended from the sort that were killed historically on Alexander Fleming's culture plate, now have a whole group of genes for resistance to several different antibiotics. And this resistance has been brought about by the antibiotics themselves, in the way we have just seen.

Luckily for us, newer and more sophisticated antibiotics, in cocktails of several at a time if necessary, are still winning the fight against the large majority of disease microbes. But we can expect the talented microbes to go on improving their drug resistance, so that it will always be a running battle.

Helpful microbes
Among the helpful microbes are the ones that make antibiotics, which chemists extract from the microbes' cells and which doctors then use as medical drugs. Microbes, particularly bacteria, can be made medically useful in another way, which can also be understood by looking at their heredity or genetics.

We have already seen that a disease bacterium may have a gene that helps it resist attack by an antibiotic drug. This happens

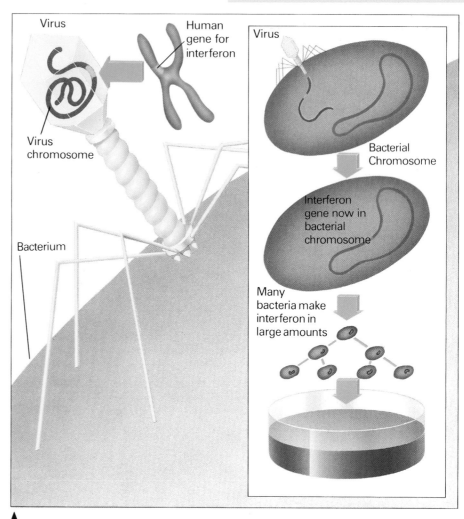

▲
The picture shows how the drug interferon can be grown in large amounts in the laboratory using a virus and a bacterium. Interferon is a powerful and non-poisonous drug, effective against disease viruses. It is made naturally by living cells, but only in tiny and very expensive quantities. The new microbe technology will make interferon and other wonder drugs much cheaper and more available.

▼
Helpful microbes include those from which we extract antibiotics, and others that we use to make food. The Japanese are the world's experts in using fungus moulds and bacteria to make special foods.

How antibiotics work. These powerful drugs either kill disease bacteria outright, or stop them from multiplying in the body. In either case, disease is prevented.

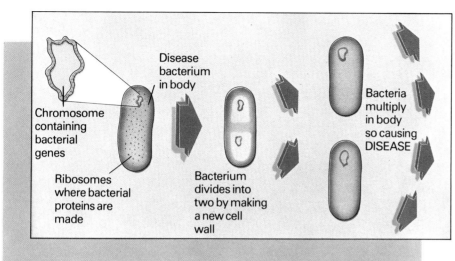

Disease bacterium in body

Chromosome containing bacterial genes

Ribosomes where bacterial proteins are made

Bacterium divides into two by making a new cell wall

Bacteria multiply in body so causing DISEASE

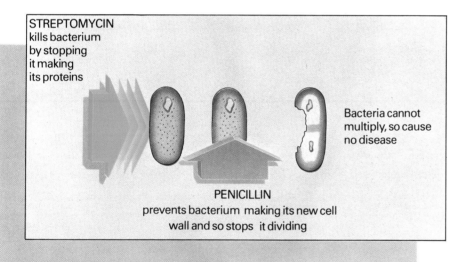

STREPTOMYCIN kills bacterium by stopping it making its proteins

Bacteria cannot multiply, so cause no disease

PENICILLIN prevents bacterium making its new cell wall and so stops it dividing

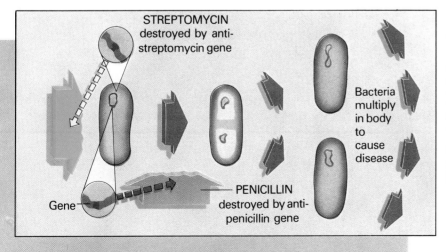

STREPTOMYCIN destroyed by anti-streptomycin gene

Bacteria multiply in body to cause disease

Gene

PENICILLIN destroyed by anti-penicillin gene

because the gene causes an enzyme to be made, which prevents the action of the antibiotic. An enzyme is a very complicated chemical compound that makes the chemical reactions of life take place in the living cells of all organisms.

Generally, one particular gene causes one particular enzyme to be made, which then causes one particular chemical reaction to take place. In the case of the bacterium's drug-resistance gene, this is certainly not to our advantage, because the chemical reaction stops the antibiotic working. But can a bacterial gene be made to turn out something not harmful, but useful, for us? The answer has been yes for many centuries. Certain bacteria, for example, make acid from alcohol, and man has long used this process to make vinegar. It is quite a natural process. Wine left around long enough will always go sour, because bacteria from the air infect the wine and use their special genes to make the acid.

In the last 30 years or so, scientists have learned how to inject new genes into a bacterium's chromosome. These new genes then make the bacterium start producing substances that it did not make before. Unlike antibiotics or vinegar, this is not a natural process. But it is a very important one for medicine, since the new substances can be vitally important drugs that cannot otherwise be made cheaply. It is such a new process that only a few drugs are as yet made this way. By the end of the 20th century, however, many once expensive drugs, as well as many still newer, unthought-of ones, will be turned out in large quantities in micro-factories by billions of dutiful bacteria.

Medical miracles

Surgical wonders

With the discovery of antiseptics, surgical operations became safe. With the invention of anaesthetics, they became painless. These two great leaps forward were made more than a century ago (see pages 24-25) but by means of modern technology, surgery is still advancing fast.

'Safe' and 'painless' are relative terms. Certainly, at the beginning of our century, a patient who had been operated on would not have suffered as much as one of 50 years before. But anaesthetics such as chloroform were fairly dangerous poisons, and infections after operations were by no means unknown.

Today, both these dangers are rare in up-to-date hospitals. Operations have been made still safer and less scary with the use of newer anaesthetics, including the 'pre-med' injection that makes you feel dopey before your operation, and the 'knock-out-drop' injection that puts you safely to sleep in a few seconds. Once under, you are watched and looked after very carefully by the anaesthetist, who supplies you with the anaesthetic gas that keeps you asleep and oblivious to pain. After the operation you are unlikely to feel any of the sickness caused by the older types of anaesthetic. After even a major internal operation, you may be up and about in only a few days.

New parts for old

Nowadays, about one person in every ten visiting a local doctor complains of joint pain, that is, pain in one or another of the parts of the body where one bone moves against another. These parts have to take the most wear and tear, so it is not surprising that they can go wrong. Middle-aged or elderly people are the most frequent sufferers, and this group is increasing in numbers as people live to a greater age.

Sometimes the doctor can offer relief without surgery, in the form

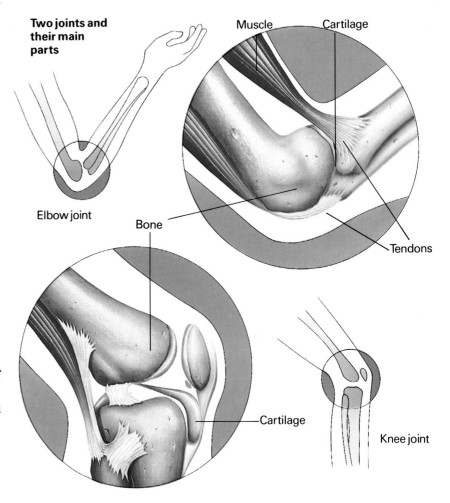

Two joints and their main parts

Elbow joint

Bone

Muscle

Cartilage

Tendons

Cartilage

Knee joint

of rest or exercise for the painful joint. One of the many pain-killing drugs now available can also be prescribed, including those that lessen inflammation inside the joint. But arthritis, as joint inflammation is called, may be so severe that besides being very painful, the complicated joint may seize up and be damaged beyond repair. At this point, a patient of 50 years ago could only look forward to a life more or less restricted by his crippling deformity. Modern surgery offers a quite different and more normal future, since the diseased joint can often be replaced with an artificial one that works perfectly well and will not wear out in the patient's lifetime.

Replacement joints are designed and made by medical engineers in tough, permanent metals, plastics and ceramics that

are quite neutral inside the body. In this way, they do not set up inflammation and a patient feels nothing unusual. Almost any joint in the body may now be replaced in this way, from the largest, such as the hip joint, to the smallest, such as the finger joints – which some hospital outpatients now have replaced while they wait! Ankle, knee and elbow joints are the most complicated in the body but are replaced by routine surgery in some very modern hospitals.

When accident or disease has robbed someone of most or all of a limb, this too can be replaced. A modern artificial arm or leg is a complicated piece of engineering, with elbow and wrist, or knee and ankle joints that their user gradually learns to control until his movements cannot be distinguished easily from those of

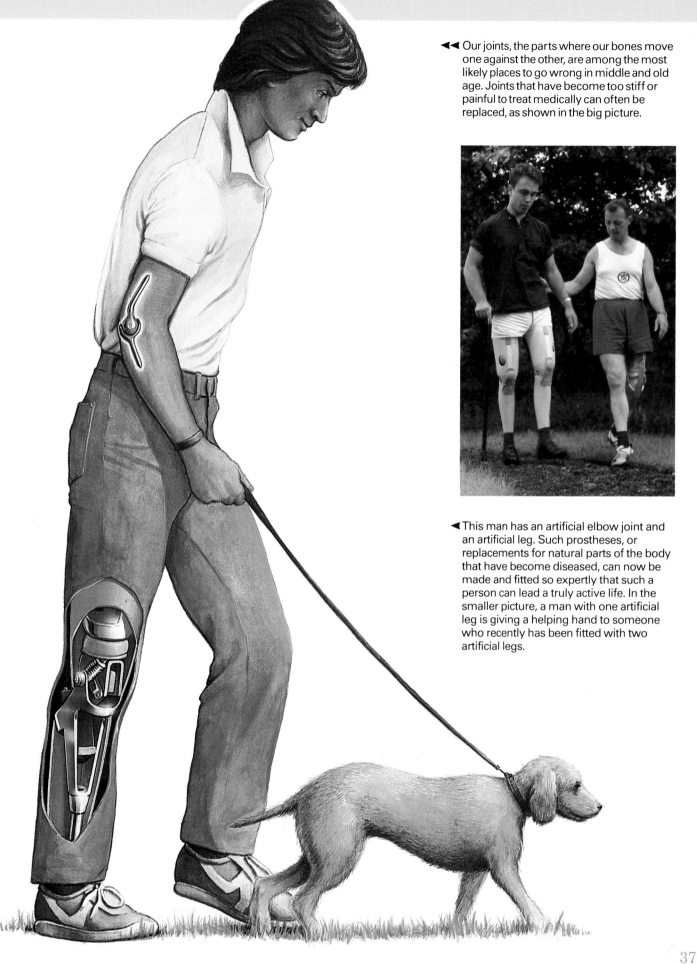

◄◄ Our joints, the parts where our bones move one against the other, are among the most likely places to go wrong in middle and old age. Joints that have become too stiff or painful to treat medically can often be replaced, as shown in the big picture.

◄ This man has an artificial elbow joint and an artificial leg. Such prostheses, or replacements for natural parts of the body that have become diseased, can now be made and fitted so expertly that such a person can lead a truly active life. In the smaller picture, a man with one artificial leg is giving a helping hand to someone who recently has been fitted with two artificial legs.

Medical miracles

an uninjured person. Artificial hands must make even more delicate movements and so are still more complicated prostheses, as the parts of replacement anatomy are called.

Transplants

In recent years, newspapers have carried stories of patients being given new hearts to replace their own diseased, worn-out ones, offering them a new lease of life. The same newspapers, sometimes weeks or months later, print smaller news items announcing the death of such patients, often from infection while they were still in hospital. These newspaper stories do, in their way, tell the truth about heart transplant operations — that they are by no means total success stories. All the same, the very ability of surgeons to transplant a vital organ from one human body into that of another person is itself a major achievement in medical science.

The most successful transplant operations so far have been those in which a dead person's cornea (the transparent window of tissue at the front of each eye) is grafted on to the eye of a patient whose own cornea has become clouded over by disease.

The almost 100 per cent success rate of this operation is explained by the fact that the cornea is a part of the body that is not supplied with blood. As explained on page 18, blood carries those parts of our defence system called antibodies, whose purpose is to get rid of foreign invaders. So, when blood is carried to any transplanted organ, the organ is likely to be attacked by antibodies in the blood. The antibodies try, often successfully, to reject the invader, a process known medically as rejection.

Doctors can overcome rejection in two main ways to allow a patient to 'accept' his transplanted organ. First, they try to choose an organ with tissues as chemically similar to his own as possible. Ideally, then, the organ would come from an identical

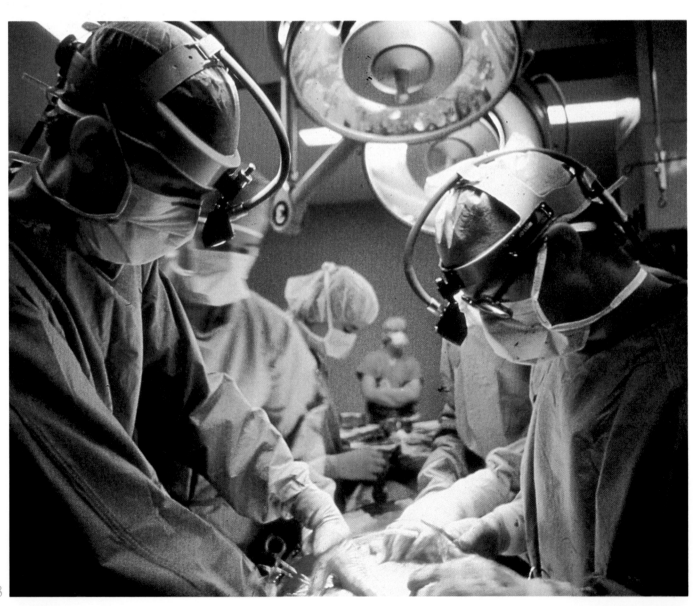

twin, but failing this unlikely possibility, from a near relative or someone unrelated who just happens to have similar tissues. This is called tissue typing.

Then, to prevent rejection of the more or less foreign tissue by the patient, the doctors give him one or more of the new drugs called immuno-suppressive drugs. These drugs suppress or discourage the action of the body's immune system, which produces antibodies.

A patient who has received a transplanted heart — or kidney or liver — may have to be kept on immuno-suppressive drugs for many months after his operation. During this time, even if his transplanted organ works healthily enough in his body, he is open to all kinds of dangerous infections because his defences are crippled by the drugs — which explains many of the sadder reports in the newspapers. However, if a patient can be kept completely free from infection, and if, as is then likely, his body learns eventually to accept the foreign organ as its own, then he can indeed look forward to years more of active life. As doctors and surgeons get to know more about the body's immensely complicated defence system, successes of organ transplants will further improve, so that by the end of our century 'a new heart' may be something more than a desperate remedy.

◄ Heart repair operations are brilliant examples of modern medical science and skill, often allowing severely ill heart patients to regain a perfectly normal, healthy life. Heart transplant operations, in which the patient receives a complete new heart from someone else's body, are even more famous. But there are many difficult health problems still to be solved before these operations become really successful.

► If a person's kidneys fail to work properly, he may die without medical help because his kidneys no longer filter out the wastes from his blood. Some kidney patients may be put on this kind of dialysis machine, which does the filtering normally carried out by the kidneys. If he is especially lucky, the patient may eventually get a successful kidney transplant.

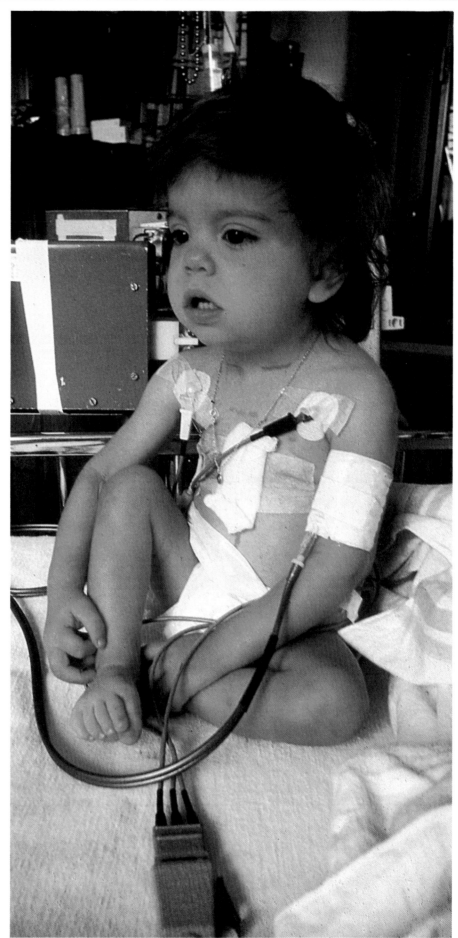

Medical miracles

Plastic surgery

Cosmetic or plastic surgery is not simply what its name implies, something to improve the shape of a film star's nose or iron out wrinkles from his or her sagging cheeks. Cosmetic surgeons do frequently carry out repairs such as these, but more often they are called upon to repair the far worse damage done to a person's appearance by a violent accident such as a car smash or a fire, or by disfiguring disease.

Often, the results of these operations seem almost miraculous, as when a cosmetic surgeon succeeds in rebuilding virtually the whole of an injured person's face. This involves transplanting or grafting skin and other tissues from different parts of the patient's body, a technique at which cosmetic surgeons have become expert. In bad burn cases, where a patient may have lost most of his skin, he has to receive tissues donated from another person, or from a 'tissue bank'. Then the immuno-suppressive drugs again become vital, to prevent rejection of the foreign tissues by the patient's body.

Another remarkable development is microsurgery, in which the surgeon makes tiny but vital repairs. With the aid of a microscope that greatly magnifies the parts the surgeon is working on, tiny microneedles can be carefully manipulated to stitch together small blood vessels. These are then able to carry blood to a part of the body which needs it badly.

On a rather similar scale are new surgical techniques of welding together small, damaged parts of the body, using heat. This may be done with a cauterizing or heating wire, or with a narrow, intense beam of energy. Lasers, which give out such beams, are used for welding back in place the small and delicate retina of the eye if this has become detached.

Medical machines

For almost a century X-rays have been used in medicine, ever since it was discovered that these rays could pass through the solid material of our bodies. The X-rays can then be made to leave an image on a photographic film or plate, in a similar way to light rays in a camera. The X-rays penetrate hard, dense tissues such as bone less well than softer tissues such as skin and muscle. So they quickly became used for imaging these harder internal parts of the skeleton, as an aid to diagnosing

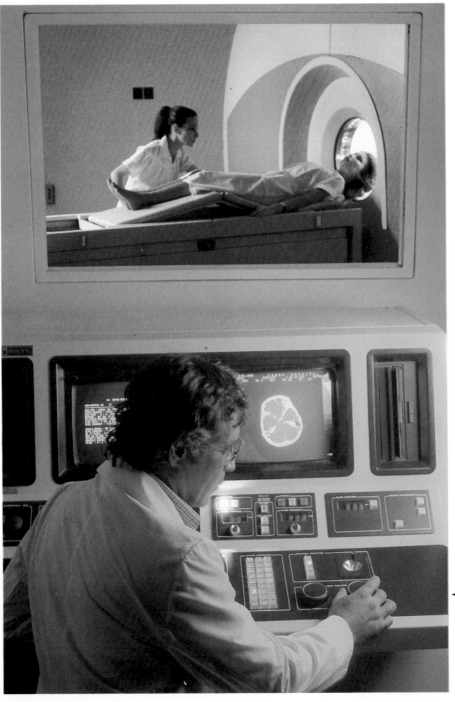

◄ Rapid sound waves can be used to 'map' a patient's entire body. In this way, the exact parts of her body affected by any illnesses such as cancer can be pinpointed. This in turn makes treatment a lot easier. The top part of the photo shows the patient's head inside the scanner. The lower part shows a cross-section or map of her skull and brain.

disease. Some chemical substances, such as barium sulphate, block out X-rays and can be given as 'barium meals' to a patient, so that soft parts such as the stomach and intestines can also be imaged by X-rays.

Large X-ray machines were soon found to be useful in the treatment of disease. The X-rays can be concentrated or focused narrowly on internal growths such as cancers and burn such growths away. This important application shows that X-rays can harm as well as cure, since they also damage healthy tissue if used improperly. Also, repeated X-ray doses might even be the cause of cancer. For this reason safer methods of imaging the internal parts of the body are being sought.

One newer method is to use very rapid sound waves, which can penetrate the body and be made to produce images, but which do less harm to tissues. Even more recent and promising is the technique called nuclear magnetic resonance or NMR, in which the patient's body is put between extremely powerful magnets. Images of the inner parts can then be obtained without passing any rays or waves through the body.

The medical machines of the near future are likely to be very small as well as very large. Miniaturized electronic units will carry out some vital task for the body. Already, electronic pacemakers can be implanted under a patient's skin to keep a bad heart beating properly. Still to be perfected are electronic transducers enabling blind people to see and the completely deaf to hear. An eye transducer will change light signals into electrical signals which will travel to the visual or seeing part of the brain. An ear transducer will convert sound signals to electrical signals and feed them to the auditory or hearing parts of the brain. And either of these units could be as small as one of today's pocket calculators.

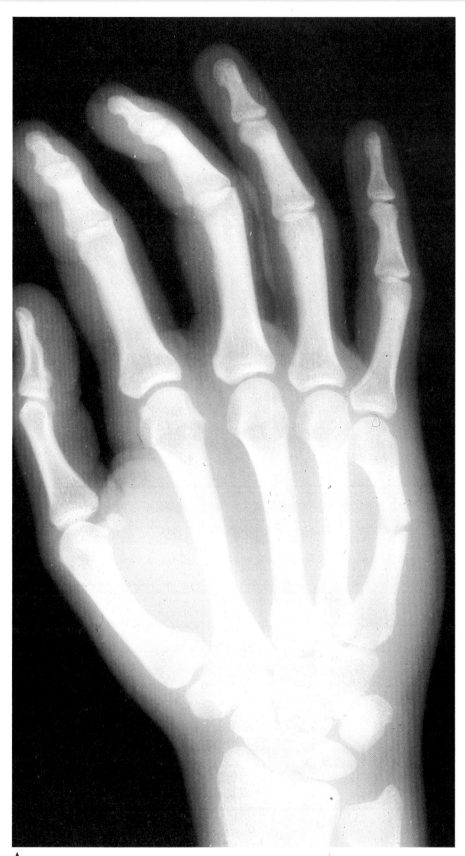

▲
This radiograph, or X-ray photograph, shows clearly how the rays penetrate softer parts of the body while showing up harder, denser parts. In this case, the X-rayed patient has a broken bone under the little finger.

CHAPTER 5
World health problems

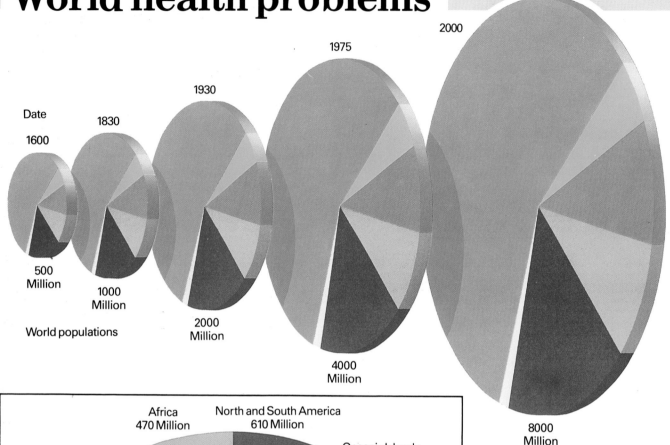

Date

1600
500 Million

1830
1000 Million

1930
2000 Million

1975
4000 Million

2000
8000 Million

World populations

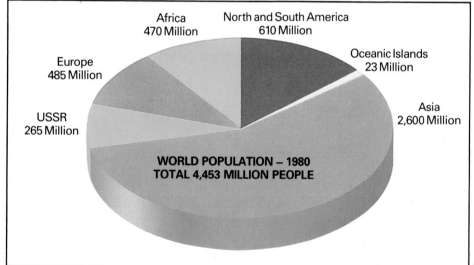

Africa
470 Million

North and South America
610 Million

Europe
485 Million

Oceanic Islands
23 Million

USSR
265 Million

Asia
2,600 Million

WORLD POPULATION – 1980
TOTAL 4,453 MILLION PEOPLE

The chart shows how world population has spiralled madly upwards in the last 150 years. One of the biggest problems facing WHO (the World Health Organization) today is that large and health-hungry countries such as Brazil and Indonesia are also the ones with the fastest-growing populations.

Let's begin with a quote: 'WHO aims to make possible for all citizens of the world, by the year 2000, a level of health that will permit them to lead a socially and economically productive life.'

WHO, or the World Health Organization, is a part of UNO, the United Nations Organization. It was formed after World War II to attack the major problems of disease worldwide. WHO is particularly concerned with those poorer countries whose people, far from leading 'socially and economically productive lives' up to now have lived in the shadow of

infectious illness and malnutrition or chronic shortages of nourishing food. These are the countries with the biggest health problems.

Sometimes they are also countries with very big and growing populations. India, for example, now has well over 600 million people, more than the whole world population in the year 1700. Many countries in Africa, South America and South East Asia are even more unhealthy to live in than India, even if they have smaller populations.

Wars and other struggles in these countries frequently make

them almost impossible to help. So how likely is it, in under 20 years, that WHO's ambition for the year 2000 will be anything like fulfilled?

WHO's campaigns
To answer this question, it is first necessary to look at what WHO has already achieved, in its short

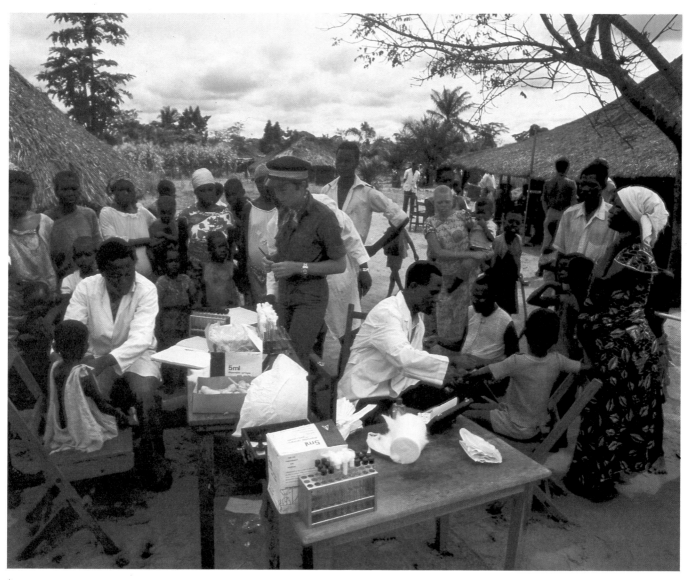

▲
The World Health Organization (WHO), sends out health teams to many needy parts of the world. But health programmes can be very costly and WHO is always short of funds. The world's nations seem more willing to spend their money on armaments than on vital health improvements.

history of less than 40 years. During this time, the organization has sent out many teams of doctors and nurses with the drugs and supplies necessary for dealing with disease emergencies worldwide. Engineers and food and welfare experts have often followed to improve food growing, sanitation and general health care in these countries in order to deal with their problems over a longer time scale.

WHO's health campaigns have often lasted ten or more years, with dramatic results.

Tuberculosis, once a great killer in the West but now a rare disease there, still ravages much of the 'Third World', as poorer countries are called when lumped together. This is a disease which is strongly linked with poverty, but against which people can be protected to a considerable extent by a vaccine called BCG. Thanks to WHO, no fewer than 100 million young people the world over have been vaccinated against tuberculosis since World War II.

Providing the people of poorer countries with a better standard of living is a more difficult matter for agencies such as WHO, which has a strictly limited budget despite the size of some of its health campaigns. Even with a membership of more than 155 countries, the organization has less to spend on health than some small countries such as Belgium, and hardly more than many of the world's richer cities. But simply by providing the people of poor countries with greater freedom from tuberculosis, WHO has enabled these people to grow more food for themselves, earn more money and so provide themselves generally with a better standard of living.

WHO's small budget has not stopped it from some startling successes in the conquest of disease. Smallpox, although a less vicious plague than in previous centuries, still killed or blinded millions of people yearly when

43

World health problems

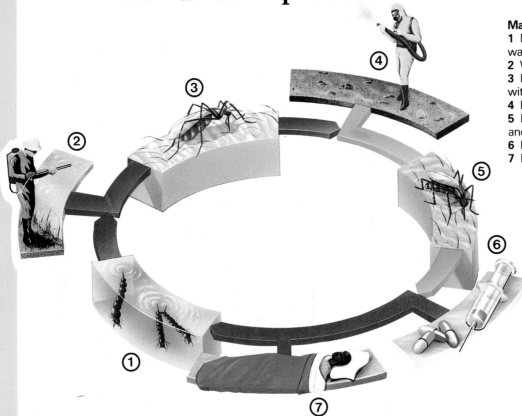

Malaria key
1 Mosquito larvae breeds in stagnant water
2 Water is sprayed with oil to kill larvae
3 Mosquito hatches and feeds on person with malaria
4 Insecticides are sprayed to kill mosquito
5 Mosquito injects malaria parasite into another person
6 People can be given anti-malarial drugs
7 Malaria still strikes

WHO moved against it in a major campaign beginning in 1967. Ten years later, not even the poorest country in the world counted smallpox as amongst the greatest threats to its health. In 1979, WHO declared the world smallpox-free. Evidence for this is that you need no longer have smallpox injections when travelling abroad.

Almost equally successful has been WHO's campaign against the tropical disease yaws. This disfiguring infection proved in the 1950s to be quickly treatable with the new wonder drug penicillin. At least 35 million people in about 40 countries were inoculated against yaws, with the result that the disease is no longer widespread in those countries. Any new case which does appear can be cured before the disease has done much damage to the patient.

Typhus is a disease that once caused millions of deaths in large-scale outbreaks or epidemics. One form of typhus killed many

soldiers in the trenches of World War I.

Even after World War II, citizens of such underdeveloped countries as Afghanistan suffered widely from typhus. The disease is spread by the bites of insects called body lice, which transfer the typhus microbes from person to person. WHO wiped out the insects and typhus microbes with DDT sprayed on to the clothing of villagers and herdsmen who attended treatment centres. DDT itself is an insecticide, or insect-killer, first made between the two World Wars.

Malaria
These are WHO's big winners in the race against disease, because the diseases in question have almost certainly been conquered on a world scale. Malaria is an infection spread by the bites of mosquitoes, insects common in hot, damp countries and still the cause of much ill-health and even mortality there. Indeed, malaria is

still so widespread in these countries that you will certainly need to take anti-malarial tablets when visiting them, to ward off the infection.

So you see that malaria can be prevented by modern drugs. The trouble for the poor countries is that drugs cost money, something that they are short of. Also, the microbe that actually causes malaria is particularly gifted at forming resistance to drugs, so that new ones keep on having to be invented - which, of course, adds further to the expense.

WHO's campaign against malaria has been one of its biggest and most complicated. First, all areas where mosquitoes are found are sprayed with insecticide. Pools and other stagnant areas of water where the insects breed may be sprayed with an oil film that prevents their grubs or larvae from breathing. By these means, malarial mosquitoes have been wiped out from whole cities or large rural areas.

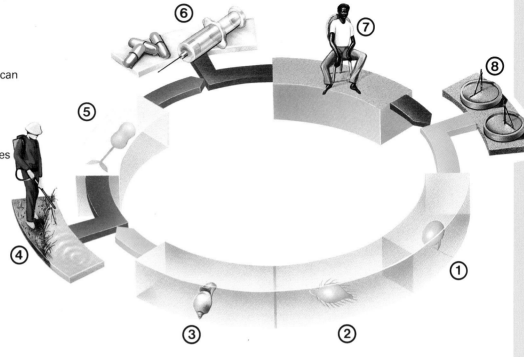

Bilharzia key
1 Human body wastes infect water with eggs of parasite
2 Egg hatches to release miracidium
3 Miracidium infects water snail
4 Water is dosed with snail-killing chemical
5 Water snail releases cercaria which can penetrate human skin
6 Patients can be treated with anti-bilharzia drugs
7 and 8 When patients suffer from bilharzia, their body waste must be prevented from reaching water supplies

▲
Malaria and bilharzia are two of the world's remaining great plagues. They both arise from infected water, as the diagrams show.

Next, a close check must be kept for any new cases of malaria occurring in these treated places. If malaria begins to increase once again among their populations, this may mean that the mosquitoes are becoming resistant to the insecticide, so that a new one will have to be tried. Luckily, insecticides are cheaper than anti-malarial drugs, so there is usually no great problem here.

The real problems WHO has faced in its global fight against malaria have resulted from the poverty and lack of development of the countries concerned. When a country has few roads on which to send out health teams, when many of its people are nomads who do not stay in any one place for very long, or when for any other reason they do not turn up regularly for treatment, then

efficient control of a complicated disease such as malaria becomes difficult if not impossible.

Bilharzia
Similar problems face health teams fighting bilharzia, another infection still threatening the

▼
Tropical forests, with their immense numbers of different plants, could provide us with many new medical drugs, including ones more natural and less poisonous than man-made drugs. But the new drugs may never be discovered. It is these richest parts of the Earth's land surface that are disappearing most quickly, where 'development' means 'destruction'.

health of hundreds of millions of people in underdeveloped countries. Control of bilharzia is even more complicated than that of malaria, because this weakening disease is spread by not one but two different small forms of animal life.

People suffer from bilharzia after they have become infected with the microscopic worms that actually cause the disease. These live in water and can penetrate the human skin, for example when a villager is bathing in a local lake. The lake water must also contain snails, in which the bilharzia worms live before they infect a human being. The snails themselves become infected because parts of the lake shore are used, for want of any better place, as toilets by the villagers. This means that the water continually gets reinfected and keeps the disease 'on the go'.

Now it is easy to see that this endemic, or 'established', infection can be tackled in several useful ways. Neither is it difficult to see that each of these ways has its special difficulties.

The villagers can be given anti-bilharzia drugs to kill the tiny parasites in their bodies. Drugs cost rather a lot for a poor country, but this will be an effective treatment, if the villagers take their drugs properly and if they do not become re-infected. Neither of which, unfortunately, is very likely.

The water snails that harbour the bilharzia parasites can be killed off with snail poison dosed into the water. This method has proved very effective in some places, but in others the lakes and swampy areas are so large that keeping them always free of snails is difficult and expensive.

Best of all would be, in the example above, if the villagers could be persuaded to change their toilet habits so that their lake did not become reinfected. But this would mean providing all of them with what you and I take for granted, efficient toilet facilities

> Where would we be without hospitals? Seriously ill or injured people may be untreatable except in a large modern hospital. But such hospitals also create human problems. In them, patients can feel lonely, cut-off and ignored.

connected to piping systems for carrying away body wastes and making these harmless. Such systems are only to be found in developed countries, so that the real cure for the bilharzia-suffering villagers is a general improvement in their standard of life.

Cleanliness and disease

Lack of clean or hygienic surroundings is a strong clue to why another disease, leprosy, has persisted in some countries, particularly India and parts of Africa. This disfiguring and crippling disease was well known and feared in ancient times, and is often mentioned in the Bible. It was common in Europe until the 13th century, when, the story goes, it vanished after the invention of linen underwear, which people changed regularly instead of wearing the same underclothes for months at a time. Whether or not this is the true reason, it is certain that the spread of leprosy depends on close contact with infected articles and persons, spread over a long time. Modern drugs are often very effective at stopping this slow but terrible affliction, particularly in children who have not yet suffered badly from it. But as with malaria and bilharzia, it is a slower and more difficult process to improve the poor general surroundings or environment that support and encourage the disease.

◄ Even well-off Europe can have its open-drains problems, as this street in Naples, Italy, shows.

► Third World hospitals are often poorly equipped. They may be able to provide little modern treatment – drugs especially may be in short supply. But usually they allow the patient's family to live in with him and keep him company.

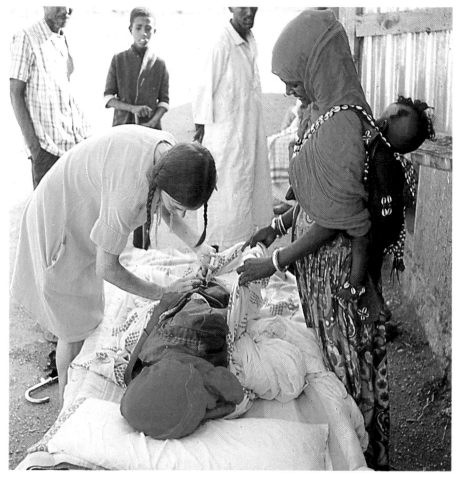

47

World health problems

The problems of want

The histories of rich industrial countries show that some of them were very different places to live in one and a half centuries ago. Now, all their citizens have, or should have, enough nourishing food to eat. Then, only the lucky rich could be said to eat well. This was true even though more food was being manufactured by the new industrial processes. The food of the industrial poor might consist entirely of factory-baked bread, weak tea, and a few boiled vegetables, with meat as an expensive rarity.

Such a meagre and unbalanced diet further weakened people whose health had already been damaged by unhealthily crowded surroundings and long factory hours. Country people of the time were often even worse off. They might breathe purer air, but they went even shorter of food. When actual starvation threatened, their misery drove them from the countryside to the cities to make these even more crowded and unhealthy. And even while most people lived so badly at this time, the population was increasing constantly. With the coming of industrialization, there were many, many more mouths to feed.

With only a few changes, this could be the story of many growing nations of the Third World today. Their agricultural labourers or peasants still flock to the cities in search of wages that will buy them enough to eat. Once there, they live miserably and unhealthily in squalid shanty towns or slums. The cities grow ever larger, their drainage and sewerage systems, if they have any to speak of, break down under the strain of enormously swollen populations, and so the nation's health problems get worse.

Of course, there are important differences from the industrial world of the early 19th century. Modern technology can solve many problems much more

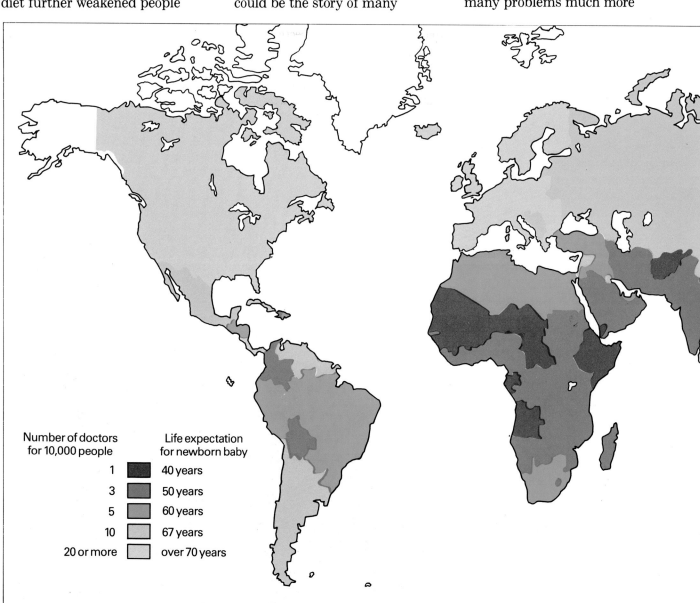

Number of doctors
for 10,000 people

Life expectation
for newborn baby

Number of doctors for 10,000 people	Life expectation for newborn baby
1	40 years
3	50 years
5	60 years
10	67 years
20 or more	over 70 years

quickly and efficiently than the technology of 150 years ago. As you can see earlier in this book, medical technology now provides a whole range of drugs and other treatments for infectious diseases, that were quite unknown at that time. So that despite their squalor and insanitary surroundings, the poorer areas of Third World cities of today are less likely to breed the sort of raging epidemics that regularly cut down the inhabitants of the crowded cities of previous centuries.

Growing populations
But if many fewer people die in epidemics, there will be many more that survive to swell populations, so providing a greater number of people to be looked after by a developing nation's health services. It is not very often that these health services are able to grow in size and efficiency to match the needs of the increasing numbers of the country's citizens.

Compared with rich countries such as the US, Japan and those of Europe, poor African and Asian countries will have only about one-tenth as many doctors, and many fewer and less modern hospitals and welfare services. This lack of health care means that in Third World countries, general ill-health is likely to be more widespread than in richer countries. One of the most distressing effects of this is the death of greater numbers of babies and young children — in some cases, ten times the number that we are prepared to tolerate in 'the affluent world'.

Third World families tend to be larger than affluent families. So one solution to the problems of the poorer, more populous parts of the world, is for their families to become smaller and so probably healthier. The quickest way for this to happen would be the use of contraceptives and other methods of birth control in the Third World. But this quick solution is really all too simple, as we shall see in the next section.

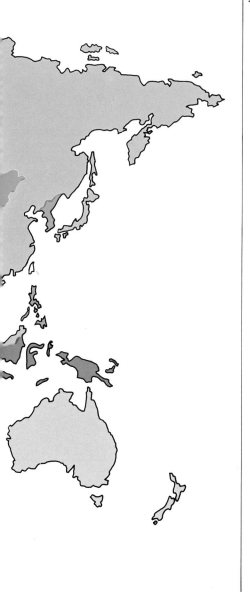

◄ The age to which you can expect to live depends on where you come from. In the poorer countries of the world, life expectation is lower, not least because more babies die. These are also the countries with fewest doctors and other medical services.

▼ In countries that have large numbers of very poor people, the average person is often quite young. This is partly the result of large families, and partly caused by high death-rates among babies and older people.

49

CHAPTER 6
Keeping healthy

The chances of a healthier world in the year 2000 can be estimated by comparing the two different worlds of today; the rich, well-fed world and the poorer, worse-fed world. The first thing to note about the poverty-stricken world is that two out of every three people live in it.

If you grow up as a typically poor inhabitant of an underdeveloped country, you are still very likely to suffer or even die from an infection such as measles. In a rich country you would be protected against measles by immunization. Indeed, in a poor country you may not live long enough to be immunized, even if you get the chance. Young babies in poor countries still die in millions from the sort of infant diarrhoea that has been eliminated from the better-off countries for over 50 years.

If you are lucky enough to avoid the worst childhood infections and get just about enough to eat, then it is likely that you will grow up to be an adult and possibly live long enough to become an old one. In adult life, too, there are vital differences between poor and rich countries. 'Old' probably means the same thing in both types of country, that is, 70 or over. But in the poor world, which has two-thirds of all people, fewer people live to be old. In Africa, for example, the average person lives to be about 50, whereas as a citizen of Europe, the US or USSR you can expect to live 20 years longer.

So far, this comparison has shown that the poorer countries have it worse all ways. The people of wealthier, developed, industrial nations get more and better food, housing and medical attention. As a result, both children and adults of the richer nations live longer than those of the poorer ones. It seems that the obvious thing to do is to convert all the poor countries into rich ones, so that their people can enjoy a better standard of life and health.

The unhealthy rich
This is a fine ambition and it is the declared aim of such agencies as WHO, as well as of the poorer nations themselves, to see it realized by the year 2000. It would be a finer ambition still, if the richer people of the world today were really all so very healthy.

Unfortunately, they are not. True, they live longer and eat better, but even this carries a new burden of disease.

As your body grows old its tissues are more likely to break down or degenerate. This can happen in many ways, among the most common of which is cancer. This is the name we give to all diseases in which cells of the body start multiplying at random, so that they do the body damage and may even kill it. Many kinds of cancer are diagnosed in ageing bodies and because old people are more often to be found in wealthier countries, so are these sorts of cancer.

As for the better diet of rich countries, there can be no doubt that this is, in itself, a good thing — except that the affluent citizens of these countries eat too much. When you eat too much, you become overweight and the fatter you are, the less likely you will be to live to a ripe old age. Even more people die in rich countries from heart disease than from cancer.

Heart disease is strongly linked with overeating, especially when combined, as it usually is, with lack of exercise. Health clubs sometimes advertise that with healthy exercise and diet, they can take the fat off rich businessmen and others who eat unwisely and too well. In a poor country, the plump person in an advertisement is more likely to represent someone healthier and better-off, someone in fact who always gets enough to eat!

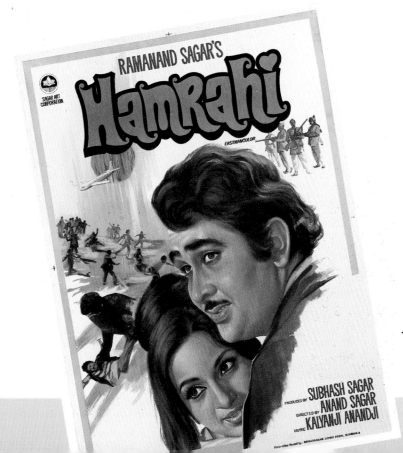

◀ In India, a country in which many people do not get enough to eat, to look plump is often to look attractive and healthy. Thinness is a sign of poverty.

▲
The stark desert area and the menacingly
crowded city both threaten the health of
their inhabitants. In bone-dry areas such as
the Sahel of Africa, the threat is obviously
one of shortage. There is too little food –
goats have nibbled away most of the green
vegetation. There is too little water – with
the disappearance of grass and trees, the
Sahara desert has moved in. City dwellers
usually have enough food and plenty of
water, but the stresses of their crowded
lives bring more mental illness.

► In affluent countries, fatness is condemned
as dangerous to health, and more and more
people are taking up fitness classes to keep
slim.

Keeping healthy

Neither heart disease nor the fatal strokes that carry off so many old people can be said to be caused by microbes, as are most of the worst killer diseases of poor countries. Nor can cancer be thought of as mainly a microbial disease, even though some forms of cancer have been shown to be caused by viruses. These three major threats to health in affluent countries are more the result of the way we live, rather than attacks from rival forms of life. Overeating helps to cause heart disease. So also does tobacco smoking, too much alcoholic drink and the stresses and strains of busy city life generally.

Smoking, particularly cigarette smoking, is rightly blamed as the major cause of cancer of the lung, the most common kind of cancer among people of rich countries. Knowing this, why do so many people continue to risk their lives by smoking? One answer is that governments, which get huge amounts of money from the tax on tobacco, are unwilling to try very hard to discourage the habit. The small government warnings on those very large cigarette advertisements have not proved very effective in getting people to stop smoking. It would be much better to ban tobacco advertising altogether!

Another, deeper reason is that smoking, like the drinking of alcohol, seems to be a way in which some people respond to the worrying demands their lives make upon them. So the illnesses caused by heavy smoking and drinking, which include forms of cancer and heart disease, can correctly be called stress or worry diseases. They are most frequent where the complications of life are worst, which is often in the richer, more industrial countries, rather than in the poorer, more rural ones.

Dangerous surroundings

Smoking tobacco is a sort of inner air pollution. The outer sorts, poisonous smogs of large cities and noxious fumes from factory chimneys, are also harmful to lungs. Smogs are caused by the build-up of traffic fumes, which contain substances known to produce cancer and brain damage. Toxic fumes from power-station chimneys ruin crops and other vegetation and cause many older people to die from bronchitis.

Besides air pollution, there is the additional threat of water pollution. In rich industrial countries, farmers can afford to use lots of chemical fertilizers to increase the growth of their crops. At least one of these chemical substances, nitrates, is suspected as a cause of cancer and heart disease. It is washed by rain off the land into rivers and lakes and so into drinking water.

These are only a few of the dangerous substances produced in ever-increasing variety and amounts by modern industry. More than likely you will have read of others, such as the horribly dangerous chemical dioxin, that caused so much damage to health when it escaped from a factory in Seveso, Italy. Of course, modern science is always good at detecting dangerous industrial chemicals and other hazards to health and explaining just why they are such a threat. But somehow this happens so often after they have accidently got out and not before.

Most dangerous of all the

everyday threats that 20th-century man has made to his own safety is road traffic. Accidents of one kind or another are the fourth biggest killer in modern society and, of these, road accidents take by far the worst toll of life. Often, many of the seriously ill patients brought into a busy hospital at night are victims of road accidents. Although these accidents all too frequently kill,

◀ The crossing that was far from safe. Road accidents now kill and injure more people in the West than all but a few diseases.

▼

The double face of a super-city. Here the industrial waste unpleasantly contrasting with the elegant city skyline is mainly an eyesore. But in the centres of high population the world over, dumping of industrial wastes has become a real threat to health.

maim or shockingly disfigure the people involved, they are nowadays so common on our roads that we have got used to them. Passing a bad accident in our car, we may stare or look away, but then soon forget about it. This reluctance to enquire further into what might be very unpleasant to look at, is 'only human nature after all' but until we do worry more about road accidents, they will go on increasing.

◀ Younger people often smoke as a way of showing that they are 'grown up'. But their mothers and fathers increasingly have stopped smoking, having convinced themselves that it is too dangerous a habit.

▼

A victim of the uncaring city lies unregarded or avoided on the pavement.

Keeping healthy

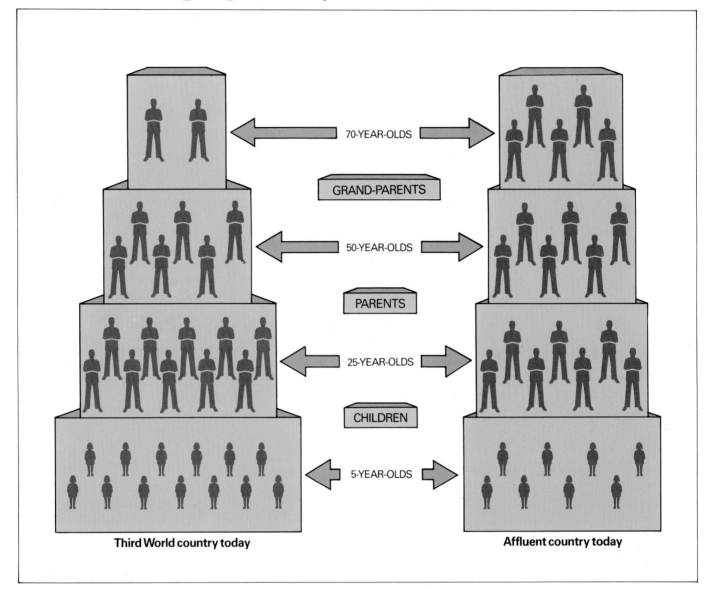

70-YEAR-OLDS

GRAND-PARENTS

50-YEAR-OLDS

PARENTS

25-YEAR-OLDS

CHILDREN

5-YEAR-OLDS

Third World country today

Affluent country today

▲
Poor, Third World families tend to be larger than those of richer countries. But fewer people in poor countries live to a ripe old age.

Caring or uncaring?
Rich societies do not always look very humane, when compared with poor ones, A huge, affluent city is the very image of uncaring, unfeeling humanity. No single human figure in the thousand-and-one streets looks at all important, as it threads its way

◀ Older people are often more respected and well cared for in Third World rural communities than in richer industrial ones. But we must always remember that these grandmothers and grandfathers are fewer in number than those of more crowded, split-up communities and so are easier to look after properly when they become aged and infirm.

through crowds and towering buildings and avoids the seething or hurtling traffic. Compare a peaceful Third World village, with little or no traffic to bother its inhabitants while they chat in the street or are seated, perhaps, under a shady tree in the village square. Obviously, each person has his or her importance here, more especially the respected village elders who, in the big city, would be among the most ignored and at risk from fast-moving cars and lorries.

This comparison is, of course, unfair. A big city offers a much greater variety of work and entertainment than a poor village. Most of its inhabitants never have to suffer hunger, as the villagers certainly will if their crops fail. Undernourishment brings bodily weakness and disease, and in a very poor village the level of infectious illness will always be higher than in a modern city. When city dwellers do fall ill, all kinds of medical and surgical treatment are usually available, but a Third World villager may not even be able to get the drugs necessary to help him back to health.

So are the big cities healthier to live in after all? On a world scale, more and more people are choosing or aiming to live in cities and the more affluently they can live in them, the better. Affluence, as we have seen already, can solve some human problems, but is inclined to create others. More food production can mean more unhealthy overweight people and more pollution. Affluent people nowadays tend to have smaller families, which is clearly a good thing in our overcrowded world. But whereas the Third World villager has his large family around him, the smaller affluent family is more often divided up, its grandparents in many cases leading lonely, cut-off lives instead of the more dignified and cared-for ones of the village.

These luckier Third-World grandparents have one big advantage and attraction — there are fewer of them than in the affluent world. So that for each old person, there will be more younger ones to share the task of looking after them. This state of affairs in turn depends on the more sinister fact that more people must have died before reaching old age. Also, it is unfortunately true that the extra deaths occur very often among young babies. In a better-off country, where infant mortality is relatively low, more people live to a ripe age. This is the same thing as saying that babies survive better in the richer, more developed countries.

▶ In terms of her money, this old lady may be much better off than the African elder in the picture opposite. She lives in a technically advanced society in which wealth and ownership are on a bigger scale than in rural Africa. But it is also a society which has many more older, often lonely, people.

Growing up handicapped

But even this advance brings its own problems. In any part of the world, one or more of every 500 babies will be born with a severe defect or handicap. Sometimes this is just physical, sometimes both mental and physical. In every case in a poor country, the handicapped baby will be less likely to survive. In countries where advanced medical care is more available, this is no longer so. Here, even the lives of very severely handicapped babies can often be saved. These babies will rarely grow up to lead normal lives. Many will have to spend most of their lives in a wheelchair, others will be confined entirely to one or another kind of hospital all their days.

▼
Modern medical knowledge is saving the lives of more and more children who would once have died young. Such handicapped children often grow up to live useful and varied lives, but they always need a great deal of care and understanding from society.

Keeping healthy

The result of this life-saving on populations is that rich countries have a greater number of damaged children than do poor countries, in which many fewer have survived. Of those that do survive, the ones with mental handicap will usually be accepted as members of their village communities, even if only as 'the village idiot'. In more developed — but not necessarily more civilized — societies, such damaged people have become no longer acceptable. They are put away in institutions, often for their own safety, because, for example, of the dangers of modern road traffic. This in itself would not be so bad, if the mental hospitals in which the children are confined were even moderately satisfactory. On the contrary, they get less money and have fewer nurses than almost any other part of the medical service.

Healthy affluence for all?

The ambition of poor, underdeveloped countries is, understandably, to become richer and, among other things, provide a better standard of medical treatment for their people. Some of the less well-off nations of today — the ones with the rather smaller problems — will achieve this by the end of our century. By their own efforts, together with some aid from richer countries, including the most modern technology, they will have become new members of the world's affluent society.

This change for the better will be more difficult for the poorer countries with the larger problems. One of their giant problems is population. You can see from the diagram on page 54 that the world's most populous countries are by no means its richest ones. China and India together have almost half the world's population, which presents these countries with huge difficulties in the provision of food and health.

Can such giant countries reduce or at least halt the growth of their populations? At the present time,

Destruction of living areas by industrial pollution

Destruction of rain forests and other important living areas

Nuclear war

Overpopulation

Malnutrition and infectious disease

the Chinese government seems to be having some success by simply forbidding its citizens to have more than one child. But in India a recent government attempt to impose birth control ended in disastrous riots. In most developing countries, birth control can only come about slowly, with the growth of affluence, as people get out of the habit of having large families and enjoy the new personal freedoms that come with a raised income.

This is what has happened already in many of the richer countries of the world. But as we have seen, it is not the whole answer, because these countries too have their health problems, some of which have actually been created by affluence. With the ending of the large family and the increase in length of life has come, in too many cases, the greater chance of loneliness and neglect in old age. The lives of younger people are so often made more, rather than less, stressful by high technology, leading to such personal disasters as drug-taking, mental illness and suicide.

These are some of the ugly faces of affluence, but we must never forget that the better standard of living made possible by modern technology is a real advantage. Who would ever return happily to the kind of life that is always under threat from infectious disease and starvation, in which one baby in ten has little chance of growing up? This is still the world of many poor countries, and it is they who have the most urgent need of modern medical science. In our own richer world, better health is something that cannot simply be bought with money or provided by the latest medical technology. We must learn to lead less stressful, drug-free lives, eat healthily and in moderation and take plenty of exercise so that we can live to a healthy old age.

◄

Health problems that will be with us in the year 2000.

57

Glossary

Anaesthetics are drugs which relieve pain. General anaesthetics put you to sleep to do this. Local anaesthetics just numb or deaden part of you.

Analgesics are drugs which relieve pain, but not usually with numbness. Aspirin and codeine are analgesics.

Antibiotics are powerful drugs against infectious microbes. They are made by microbes themselves – usually fungi or bacteria. These microbes are grown in large numbers and the antibiotics are then extracted from their bodies. Penicillin is extracted from the common blue or green fungus mould called *Penicillium*.

Antibodies are made by certain kinds of white blood cells. They are complex *protein* molecules which attach themselves to the bodies of microbes and other foreign particles, so helping the body to get rid of these harmful invaders. Antibodies are an important part of the body's defence or *immune system*.

Antiserums are drugs that contain *antibodies* against disease. They are made usually by injecting disease microbes into the bodies of animals, which then make antibodies against the microbes. The antiserum is then extracted from the animal's blood. All this can be done without causing the horse, goat or other animal too much pain or discomfort.

Bacteria are microbes whose bodies consist of a single, microscopic cell. If a thousand bacteria were laid end to end, they would only be between one millimetre and two centimetres long. The bacterial cell may have one or more flagella (microscopic hairs) which it beats to propel itself along. Together with viruses, bacteria are the main causes of infectious disease. Very many bacteria though, are not only harmless but are vital to the balance of nature.

Blood carries nourishment and oxygen to the tissues of the body and carries wastes away from the tissues to be passed out or excreted from the body. Blood consists of two main parts: a complex liquid called plasma and the blood cells which float in this liquid.

Blood cells include red blood cells or erythrocytes (about 5,000,000 to each millilitre of blood) and white blood cells or leucocytes, (between 5000 and 10,000 to each millilitre of blood). The red cells carry oxygen from the lungs to the tissues. The white cells are mostly active in the body's defence or *immune system*.

Blood system or circulatory system is all the arteries, veins and other smaller blood vessels of the body, together with the heart that pumps blood through them.

Cancer is the name of many different illnesses or diseases, all of which have one thing in common. Cells of the body, instead of growing to the body's normal pattern, begin to multiply in a random fashion. They may go on to spread throughout the body and cause a fatal illness.

Cells are the smallest living units of the body. Our bodies consist of thousands of millions of cells. A bacterium, at the other end of the scale, has only one. *(See also Viruses.)*

Chemotherapy is the use of man-made drugs, which are special kinds of chemicals, to cure disease. *(See also Herbal medicine.)*

Chromosomes are thread-like parts of living cells. They are found in the nucleus of a cell, and they contain all or most of the cell's genes.

Deficiency diseases are those caused by lack of vitamins. An example is rickets, caused by lack of vitamin D. Bow-legged, ricketty children were common in 19th-century city slums, due to lack of sunlight and good food. Nowadays, deficiency diseases are common only in poor Third World countries. (*See also Malnutrition.*)

Digestive system is the digestive canal together with all the *glands* that aid in the digestion of food. It includes the oesophagus (the tube from throat to stomach), the stomach and its glands, the small intestine and its glands, the liver and the gall bladder. Most digested food passes into the bloodstream from the small intestine. In the large intestine, water from undigested food is absorbed back into the body.

Drug resistance of disease microbes happens when the microbes are exposed to a drug for too long a time or when the drug is too dilute or weakened to kill the microbe. The microbe then learns how to deal with the drug to make it ineffective. Doctors combat drug resistance by using more than one drug at a time or by giving newer, more effective drugs.

Endemic disease is infectious disease that is always around, waiting for the opportunity to cause serious trouble or *epidemics*. Examples in wealthy countries include some venereal diseases and common colds. Third World countries, unfortunately, still have many more endemic diseases than affluent countries.

Endocrine system is all the glands of our bodies that make hormones. These include the pituitary gland close to and below the brain, the thyroid and parathyroid glands, the pancreas, the adrenal glands, the testes in boys and men, and the ovaries in girls and women.

Enzymes are complex body chemicals, types of *proteins,* which play a vital part in body chemistry. In nearly every one of the tens of thousands of chemical reactions in the body, enzymes are necessary to make the reaction work.

Epidemics are widespread outbreaks of infectious disease. Most people have suffered at one time or another during a 'flu (influenza) epidemic. In the past, vast epidemics, or pandemics, raged across the world. The most infamous of these is plague or the Black Death.

Excretory system rids the body of its wastes. These are made as the result of chemical reactions in the body, including those occurring during the breakdown of food and worn-out tissues. The chief organs of excretion are the kidneys, which produce urine as the waste material; the skin, which excretes wastes as sweat; and the lungs, which breathe out waste carbon dioxide gas.

Genes are the units of *heredity.* Your genes caused you to have all the individual characteristics you were born with and also control your development as you grow up.

Genetics is the science that deals with the ways in which living organisms inherit their characteristics from their parents. (*See also Heredity.*)

Genetic engineering is a 20th-century branch of science by which the inherited characteristics of living organisms can be changed at will. Mostly, these organisms are microbes such as bacteria. By altering their genes, or giving

them new ones, scientists enable the microbes to perform new and useful tasks.

Germ is a popular name for any kind of disease microbe.

Glands are parts of the body that make special substances. Stomach glands make acid and *enzymes,* endocrine glands make *hormones.* The biggest gland in the body is the liver, which performs many different tasks.

Handicap means disability. A person may be born and grow up with either a physical or a mental handicap or both. A handicapped person is at risk and so any civilized country will look after its handicapped citizens.

Health services include hospitals, ambulances, local health clinics and government health advice departments. A few lucky countries have a national health service that looks after rich and poor alike. These include Sweden and Britain.

Herbal medicine uses drugs made or extracted from plants. Most famous is Chinese herbal medicine, 3000 years old and with many thousands of herbal remedies.

Heredity is the passing-on of characteristics from parents to offspring. The parents' genes contain all the information that leads to the birth and physical development of their children.

Hormones are chemical messengers carried in the blood, and control many of the ways in which the body works. They are made by the endocrine *glands.*

Immune system is the internal defence system of the body. It is extremely complicated and is only partly understood even by immunologists. Its most important parts are the

antibodies and the blood cells that make them, and other sorts of white blood cells that act against foreign invaders such as disease microbes.

Infection is the penetration of the body by microbes that can set up disease.

Inoculation is deliberately infecting a person, usually by injection, with a mild case of a serious disease. This protects against a future attack by the illness.

Lymphocytes are types of white blood cells vital to the body's *immune system.* They include cells which make *antibodies.*

Malnutrition means not enough good food. A person can suffer from malnutrition in several ways. Starvation is extreme malnutrition or lack of food. Lack of vitamins causes *deficiency diseases.* Lack of protein causes wasting disease. All these types of malnutrition are common in very poor underdeveloped countries.

Microbes are forms of life too small to be seen with the naked eye but visible through a microscope. They include protozoa (one-celled 'animals'), algae (microscopic 'plants'), very small fungi, bacteria, and viruses.

Microsurgery is surgical repair of the body on a very small scale. The surgeon uses a microscope to see the parts he is operating on and uses microneedles to stitch up such small parts as blood vessels.

Muscle system is all the muscles of the body. These are of two main types. Most familiar are the skeletal muscles that allow us to stand, walk, breathe and make other 'intended' movements. Less obvious are the smooth muscles which carry out many movements inside our bodies without our conscious decision.

Nervous system is the brain together with all the nerves of the body. The central nervous system is the brain plus all the nerves that carry conscious messages, such as those to the skeletal muscles. The autonomic nervous system is all those nerves that carry unconscious messages, such as those to the smooth muscles of the body. These two parts of the nervous system are closely linked together.

Organs are distinct parts of the body that carry out special tasks. Examples are the kidneys, which filter out body wastes, and the skin, which is the outermost barrier against infection and is also an organ of temperature control.

Pacemaker is a small electronic device (smaller than a wafer pocket calculator) that is fitted under a heart patient's skin to keep his bad heart beating regularly, by means of tiny, regular electronic shocks.

Phagocytes are white blood cells that move around and nearby tissues, gobbling up bacteria and other foreign invaders of the body.

Plastic surgery or cosmetic surgery, is repair of the body to improve its appearance and remove unsightly features. It ranges from beauty treatment such as the straightening-out of a crooked nose, to major body repairs such as those necessary after a motor accident or a fire.

Prosthesis (plural prostheses) is any artificial part that is fitted on or in the body to replace a missing part and carry out its work. False teeth and artificial joints and limbs are prostheses.

Proteins are complex chemical molecules that are vital parts of all living organisms. Meat or flesh is largely protein, together with some fat. Other kinds of proteins in the body are the *antibodies* of the blood and the *enzymes* that enable most chemical reactions to take place.

Rejection in medical terms, is the body's refusal to accept foreign parts such as tissues and organs transplanted into the body.

Reproductive system is all the parts of the body concerned with the production of babies. In the man, these are the penis and the testes (that make sperm). The woman's reproductive organs are the ovaries (that make eggs or ova), the womb or uterus (that holds the unborn baby) and the vagina (the canal through which the baby is born).

Spores are microscopically tiny parts of bacteria, moulds and other lowly organisms. Spores enable them to reproduce, rather in the way of the seeds of higher plants.

Strokes in medicine, are illnesses caused by the bursting of one or more blood vessels in the brain. This can cause paralysis, loss of consciousness or mental confusion. Strokes are common among very old people.

Third World is all those countries in which the mass of the people have barely enough, or not enough, to live on.

Tissues are parts of the body with special types of cells and functions. A body organ usually contains several types of tissues.

Tissue banks are special medical units in which tissues separated from the body are kept alive, for *transplant* purposes.

Toxins are poisons made by disease microbes. In the body's *immune system*, toxins are destroyed or neutralized by antitoxins made in the same way as *antibodies*.

Transplants in surgery, are organs from one person used to replace a diseased or missing organ in another person's body. Heart, kidneys, liver and skin are among transplants that can now be made with at least some success.

Ulcer is a part of the body, usually fairly small, where the tissues have died to leave a saucer-like hollow. Mouth ulcers are common examples. Some tropical ulcers are larger and more serious.

Vaccination is another name for immunization by inoculation or injection. See page 20 for the way the name vaccination first came about.

Vaccines are drugs that contain weakened or killed microbes or their products, which cause the body's *immune system* to make *antibodies* against infection with these particular microbes.

Viruses are the smallest kinds of infectious microbe and the only kinds that are non-cellular (not made up of one or more cells). All viruses need a living cell in which to reproduce themselves, so that they are all parasites (live off) other organisms. Many viruses cause disease.

Vitamins are substances in food that the body must have to remain healthy, although it needs them only in small amounts. Lack of vitamins leads to *deficiency diseases*.

X-rays are very penetrating forms of radiation (light and heat are less penetrating forms) which can be made to pass through the body and leave a photographic record of the body's insides.

Index

Page numbers in *italics* refer to relevant illustrations and captions.

Picture acknowledgements

All-sport 17 bottom **British Small Animal Veterinary Association** 22 **Camerapix Hutchison** 2 bottom, 4 top right, 4 bottom, 6 top, 9 bottom, 20-21, 29 bottom, 44-45, 45, 47 bottom, 49, 54, 56 bottom, 57 centre **Colorsport** 2-3, 12 **Anne Cope** 29 top right **Daily Telegraph Colour Library** 7, 9 top, 13, 47 top, 55 bottom, 57 bottom **Dista Products** 31 top, 62 bottom **Mary Evans Picture Library** 2 top, 21 **Explorer** 33 top right **The Mansell Collection** 27 **Multimedia Publications** 32, 40, 52, 53 top, 53 bottom right, 62 left **Museum of London** 20 **Oxfam** 51 top left **Rex Features** 1, 9 right, 10, 38, 51 bottom, 55 top, 58 top **St. Mary's Hospital Medical School** 33 left **Science Photo Library** 3, 4 top left, 6 bottom, 18, 33 bottom right, 39, 41, 57 top **Vision International** 14, 17 top, 23, 24, 30, 34, 46, 51 top right, 53 bottom left, 58 bottom **John Watney Photo Library** 6 centre, 6-7, 26-27, 31 bottom **ZEFA** 10-11, 29 top left, 37, 56 top, 58 right

Artwork by Mulkern Rutherford and **John Strange**

Multimedia Publications (UK) Limited have endeavoured to observe the legal requirements with regard to the suppliers of photographic and illustrative materials.